KE
URBAN
LEGENDS

KENT
URBAN
LEGENDS

THE PHANTOM HITCH-HIKER
AND OTHER STORIES

NEIL ARNOLD

The
History
Press

This book is dedicated to Terry Cameron
– a good friend

First published 2013

The History Press
The Mill, Brimscombe Port
Stroud, Gloucestershire, GL5 2QG
www.thehistorypress.co.uk

British Library Cataloguing in Publication Data.
A catalogue record for this book is available from the British Library.

ISBN 978 0 7524 8146 3

Typesetting and origination by The History Press
Printed in Great Britain
Manufacturing managed by Jellyfish Solutions Ltd

CONTENTS

	Acknowledgements	7
	Foreword	8
	Introduction	11
one	Bloody Mary	21
two	The Phantom Hitch-hiker	28
three	The Necessary Evils of Modern Technology	58
four	Devilish Legends	69
five	School Legends	92
six	If You Go Down to the Woods (and Water) Today	112
seven	More Strange Urban Legends	145
	Bibliography	191

ACKNOWLEDGEMENTS

WITH MANY THANKS to my mum, Paulene; dad, Ron; sister, Vicki; wife, Jemma; nan, Win; granddad, Ron; Sean Tudor; Joe Chester; Terry Cameron; Janet Bord; *Fortean Times*; Paul Langridge; Kent Online; *Evening Post*; *Chatham Standard*; Medway Archives; Richard Freeman; Nick Redfern; The History Press; Corriene Vickers; the *Daily Mail*; the *Sun*; the *Telegraph*; the *Guardian*; Missy Lindley; Centre For Fortean Zoology; Simon Wyatt; Charlie Ford; the *Washington Post*; *Kent Today*; *Kentish Express*; Jackie Grebby; *Gentleman's Magazine*; the *Daily Mirror*; *The Times*; *East Kent Mercury*; Public Ledger; *Medway Messenger*; *South London Times*; *New York Mirror*; *Sittingbourne Messenger*; *Dartford Messenger*; Pam Wood; and Alex Wilson.

Illustrations by Simon Wyatt (except those on pp. 28 and 145 which are by the author).

FOREWORD

NEIL ARNOLD'S LATEST book contains many tales that would have seemed extraordinary to me as a child. I grew up in rural Leicestershire in the 1950s and attended a typical village school. We did have our superstitious beliefs, of course, such as holding the corner of your collar if an ambulance raced past (presumably to ensure it didn't stop for you next time), and not stepping on the cracks in a pavement or walking under a ladder, both of which brought bad luck. But I recall no talk of 'urban legends' or 'foaf-tales', and the only spooky phenomena I was aware of at that time were ghosts and hauntings. These definitely did intrigue me, but little did I know that one day I would research and write about them!

The best-known haunting in our neighbourhood was the White Lady, who had been seen more than once on the main road which passed the eerie ivy-clad ruins of a nunnery. She was thought to be a phantom nun, and it has been discovered that the nuns there did wear white habits. There have been numerous sightings of her over the years, but strangest of all was the time in 1954 when a bus driver stopped to pick up a lady in white standing at the bus stop opposite the nunnery, who vanished when the door was opened. So we very nearly had our own phantom hitch-hiker – though not nearly so dramatic as some of the hitch-hiker stories told here by Neil.

His chapter on modern technology contains stories that could not possibly have been told in the 1950s, since we had no modern technology at all! If you had a telephone and a television (black and white only, of course), you were considered very advanced; microwaves, computers, mobile phones, etc., would have been the stuff of science fiction. Of course the present-day ease with which everyone can keep in touch and informed probably means that urban legends spread much more quickly than ever before; and new ones are surely being invented all the time by people with lively imaginations. However, the sheer variety of historical tales which Neil also recounts shows that people have always delighted in passing on weird and frightening stories, even when the only means of transmission was word of mouth, and it's part of human nature to want to frighten people in this way.

Once I started my own research into these fields, beginning with *Mysterious Britain* in 1972, I soon realised that my childhood reading into the weird and wonderful had not extended very far at all. Apart from some collections of ghost stories, no books on mysteries had come my way, not even through the small local library which I visited weekly. Today's children are much better served – though whether an early acquaintance with some of the most scary tales is a good thing, I am not at all sure! Over the years I have researched and written about a wide range of mysteries, from the folklore of ancient sites (in *The Secret Country* and *The Atlas of Magical Britain*, for example) to reports of mystery animals worldwide (in *Alien Animals* and *Bigfoot Casebook*). I don't think I was hampered by having missed out on reading this kind of material when I was a child; but on the other hand, to have heard about more local mysteries than just the phantom White Lady would have enlivened my childhood no end! Knowing how much research is involved in putting a book like this together, I have to congratulate Neil on the extent of the research he has undertaken, and I am envious of the ease with which the people of Kent can now find out about the wealth of mysteries and spooky places they have close at hand.

Janet Bord, 2013

INTRODUCTION

Now let's take another story, this one an oral tale of the sort that never has to be written down. It is simply passed mouth to mouth, usually around Boy Scout or Girl Scout campfires after the sun has gone down and marshmallows have been poked onto green sticks to roast above the coals.

✦

Danse Macabre, Stephen King

RESEARCHER DAVID EMERY defines an urban legend as 'An apocryphal, second-hand story told as true and just plausible enough to be believed'. In other words, these friend-of-a-friend tales (foaf-tales) are passed down through generations and told as fact, despite a lack of evidence to support them. I spent thirty years of my life growing up in the town of Chatham, in Kent, and such local legends were rife – as they are all across the world – and the most amazing thing about some of the more bizarre stories was the fact that people actually believed them, despite the tales being full of holes. In turn, the believability of such yarns meant that they became embedded in local history and folklore, tattooed on the human psyche for generations to come. These tales (some more credible than others) depicted unusual events, ranging from the downright comical to the horrifying and absurd. Some legends were complex in their nature, others short and simple, and yet each one was potent enough to squirm into the subconscious mind, where it would lay dormant until the next time some rumour or incident ignited its spark.

Urban legends are powerful because one seemingly banal story can last not just a few days but a few decades, rolling off the tongue of many a storyteller in varying guises. Urban legends don't just have the ability to take over a household, but an entire town, as, like Chinese whispers, they are passed from person to person and gradually altered over time to fit in with the current climate. Urban legends can cause panic, hysteria and confusion. For example, one of the best-known urban legends worldwide concerns a phantom known as The Hook. This story is predominant in American legend and spooked me as a kid. It is told as follows:

A young couple are driving late at night, hoping to find a secluded spot to 'make out'. They reach an isolated area – a dark, wood-enshrouded lane – and pull over into a lay-by. The couple start to chat, staring lovingly into each other's eyes. The moon is leering down, bathing the vehicle in an eerie glow, the spindly trees reaching towards the vehicle. The young woman is rather spooked by the surroundings, despite the close affections of her aspirant lover. She tells him that there's been a rumour throughout High School that some of the more deserted spots of the town are being frequented by a prowler who has a hook in place of one of his hands – hence the name, The Hook. According to the tale, the sinister stranger (possibly an asylum escapee) lingers outside parked vehicles occupied by young, cavorting couples. Of course, the hot-blooded male scoffs at such a story, and attempts to make a move on the young woman. She asks, for the sake of comfort, if they can have the radio on; the silence outside is making the looming shadows all the more eerie. The male obliges, flicking on the radio and adjusting the dial to find a suitable station. Suddenly, they hear on the radio a story concerning a man – with a hook for a hand – who has been seen in the neighbourhood where they are now parked. Naturally, the news terrifies the girl, and, according to the urban legend, the couple suddenly hear a sound outside the car – a tap, tapping on the window maybe? The young lady is so unnerved that the man decides to drive her home. He starts the car and they head off into the night. But when the woman slips out of the car, she notices, to her utmost horror, a hook dangling from the door handle. And so it seems that the couple had a lucky escape from the phantom.

Now, this is quite a creepy story, and one passed round American high schools, colleges, and the like for many years, mainly since the 1950s. However, the story of The Hook is nothing more than an urban legend; a tale that has slipped through several generations as a warning to couples not to make out in remote corners of their respective counties. Although such a tale would make for a great horror film, the facts of the legend are absent as it is always difficult, if not impossible, to find an actual couple that this has happened to. But when this myth was being circulated, you could guarantee that there was always someone who knew someone else who knew a couple who allegedly had experienced it. And that is the power of the legend. Another thing that always baffled me about The Hook story was the detail concerning the actual hook, often said to have been found dangling from the door handle. If a serial killer or local weirdo had such an artificial limb, then why on earth in every case would he leave it hanging from a car door? Even as a sinister calling card, the discarded hook would suggest that this elusive character had a cupboard full of hooks to replace those he left dangling! However, in the case of The Hook we are not meant to dwell on such details but instead revel in the absolute dread the tale causes.

Over the years, and throughout the world, the tale of The Hook has varied. I recall in the 1980s a similar story from Kent. It was a vague incident recalled by a friend of a friend, who stated that one stormy night – as is always the case – around Halloween (which also helps the atmosphere of the yarn!) a couple were parked up on a remote country lane somewhere in rural Ashford. The young, testosterone-fuelled male was eager for more than a kiss on this blustery night, but his lover had heard rumours of a masked man who liked to sit in the woods alongside this stretch of road and watch couples canoodling in their vehicles. Of course, in the story, the young man is quick to quash any such tales and is eager to make a move on his date for the night. However, after a few minutes the woman notices a fleeting shadow outside the car window and so the man, being very brave in order to impress the woman, decides to investigate the surrounding foliage. As in many a horror film, the young man doesn't return and the woman becomes very scared – especially when she hears a banging sound on the roof of the car (in other versions the woman is said to hear a scratching/scraping noise on the roof).

The woman is terrified, but to her relief a police car pulls up fifty or so yards away. An officer climbs out of the vehicle and, with a megaphone, orders the woman to get out of the car slowly but to not look back. The woman leaves the car, tears streaming down her face, but despite her fit of terror she cannot resist and, when a few yards away from the car, she decides to look back. Now, there are two ends to this urban legend, depending on who you hear it from. Both are macabre. In one version – which I heard – the young woman looks back and sees the corpse of her lover hanging from a tree above the car; in the wind his mutilated body is swaying and his toes are just about caressing the roof of the vehicle, making a scraping noise. In the more over-the-top version of the legend, the woman looks back and sees a serial killer (or, in more dramatic versions, a monster) on top of the car, smashing the head of her boyfriend onto the roof. All very morbid, and all untrue, but what a great story!

And so, this is how an urban legend works, and if powerful and detailed enough such a yarn can last for several generations. The Boyfriend's Death and The Hook seem to walk hand-in-hand with their grim appeal. The story is made believable when the storyteller mentions that he knows someone it happened to, but often the location is rather vague; if you ask the narrator where it happened, in most cases they will respond, 'On a dark rural lane not far from here …', without ever giving the name of a road or nearby location. The vagueness still adds to the atmosphere of the story because, let's face it, woods, country roads and the darkest corners of our hometowns are perfect for ghost and horror stories.

Many people ask if there is any truth behind the stories and in most cases the answer to this would be a resounding no. But I've often thought that surely such bizarre stories must have an origin, and not all can be the product of a storyteller. One American story which really spooked me as a youngster concerns a terrifying legend known as the Bunnyman. Okay, so the name doesn't sound as eerie as the dreaded Hook, but bear with me. The Bunnyman legend concerned a railroad overpass situated in Fairfax County, Virginia, where every year, or so they say, local teenagers would gather at a spot known as Bunnyman Bridge. On dark nights the gangs would smoke, drink, and generally do what a lot of teenagers do, and as the area succumbed to darkness they would spin campfire tales of the dreaded Bunnyman. The Bunnyman was said to be a sum of many grisly parts. The phantom, according to some, was a recluse who lived in the woods somewhere and practised black magic. The hermit was said to have killed animals and often wore their fur (hence the name Bunnyman); he was eventually admitted to a lunatic asylum. Legend has it that the man escaped the ward and returned to the deep thickets of Fairfax County, where, adorned in rabbit skins, he would pick off local teenagers and campers with an axe. A more surreal version states that some parents in the area believed the Bunnyman to be a giant rabbit that approached children and gave them candy.

Hysterical parents, who'd grown up with tales of the Bunnyman, told their children not to trespass in the deep woods because the Bunnyman would get them. Anyone caught by the maniac would find themselves strung up dead in the trees like a morbid Christmas decoration. Another version of the Bunnyman legend states that one Easter, many years ago, a boy dressed up as an Easter bunny and killed all his family before hanging himself from the local bridge. Teenagers who tell this story claim that the legend dates back to the early 1900s and that more than thirty people over the years have been found hanging from the bridge on stormy nights. This version has, gradually, changed into another account which claims that a local hermit once killed a couple of children after he caught them trespassing on his land. Legend has it that their bodies were found hanging from the bridge.

Bunnyman has many different origins attached to it – mainly because it's not true – and one can see why it has stood the test of time, and yet bizarrely, during the autumn of 1970, the *Washington Post* reported 'Man in bunny suit sought in Fairfax', after a man – you guessed it, dressed in a white bunny outfit – allegedly attacked vehicles by throwing hatchets through the windows! The newspaper added that an Air Force Academy Cadet named Robert Bennett was sitting in his car with his fiancée in Guinea Road when 'a man dressed in a white suit with long bunny ears' emerged from the undergrowth and screamed at the car, 'You're on private property and I have your tag number.'

The 'rabbit' then threw a wooden-handled hatchet at the car, smashing the window on the right-hand side. Weirder still, two weeks later a man dressed in a bunny suit and wielding an axe was seen chopping away at the roof support of a new house built on Guinea Road. Again, the Bunnyman warned onlookers that people should not be trespassing.

Although the legend of the Bunnyman may have originated many years previously, it's intriguing how one or two unusual incidents can add to an already boiling cauldron of curiosity. Like many urban legends, there seems to be a moral. Whatever you do, don't trespass in the woods or the Bunnyman will get you! Teenagers who know of the legend also state that on no occasion should you say the name of the Bunnyman more than three times, or he will track you down. This version was echoed in a 1992 American horror film called *Candyman*. The promotional poster for the film read: 'We dare you to say his name five times.'

Although we don't realise it, such legends are around us all the time, and from a young age. Father Christmas, the Tooth Fairy, the Sandman, and the Yawning Man are four mythical figures which, in a sense, are legends passed down through generations. For instance, Father Christmas may seem to be a nice, cosy, rosy-cheeked chap keen to deliver presents on Christmas Eve, but the moral of such a legend is that if you don't behave then Santa will not come. In the case of the Tooth Fairy, parents always said that, when a tooth fell out, one should put it under the pillow; the next day, in place of the grisly item, there'd be a shiny penny. It may be my imagination but I hated the Tooth Fairy as a child. I envisaged the night creature not as an archetypal fairy with wings, a whitish hue and a wand, but in fact a black, spindly figure holding a sack full of gory, bloody teeth. I didn't want to leave my teeth for that despicable wraith because I did not want to wake in the morning knowing that the hideous thing had been in my room rummaging under my pillow. The fact that today I still have all my browning milk teeth in a little box is proof that I never trusted the Tooth Fairy!

I never trusted the Sandman either – some ghoulish entity my parents told me about which would frequent the bedrooms of children and sprinkle sand in their eyes. I also recall that if my sister, when she was little, was half-tired of a night but fighting against it, my dad would sing, whilst pretending to yawn, the following lines:

I am the Yawning Man, the Yawning Man
I yawn and I yawn all day … oh oh oh

Apparently, singing this made people yawn and want their bed. My sister and I always saw the Yawning Man as another anti-hero bogeyman, crawling from the closet into our nightmares, and we preferred to stay awake!

In more macabre urban legends the keyword is certainly 'bogeyman', and, as you will read in this book, the bogeyman pops up in many different guises, because to some extent the point of the urban legend is to warn us, and keep us safe from tragedy, misadventure and horror. A selection of modern films have used the urban legend scenario to great effect, the eeriest of these being the flick *Ring*, released in 1998. The film draws inspiration from a Japanese folk tale concerning a videotape passed between teenagers. In the film, those who view the disturbing video (which shows a female apparition rising from an old well), receive a phone call afterwards and are then found dead, frozen with fear, killed by some supernatural force. The best way to avoid death is not to view the tape, but it seems that many people are too engrossed by the legend not to believe it and so the idea of this horror is passed on, spreading like wildfire. Another film which looked at varying urban legends, also released in 1998, was the aptly named *Urban Legend*. In this American movie, a serial killer uses different urban legends to act out his grim fantasy. American urban legends such as The Killer in the Backseat, The Boyfriend's Death, and numerous others are highlighted.

Of course, not all urban legends are scary; some are fun and some are seemingly pointless – as you'll read. I've written this book as a glimpse into the urban legends that have littered the county of Kent. Some stories are very similar to those mentioned in American folklore; others are possibly unique to England. Hopefully this book will show how urban legends – and there are literally hundreds of them – are around us all the time; in our homes, schools and sprawling from the dark woods, and also in the most unlikely locations, whether it's the garage forecourt or the school playground. I'm sure too that by the time you've finished reading this book you'll relate to quite a few of the stories and probably be slightly disappointed that some of the 'true' tales you've been told, by a friend of a friend, are nothing more than legend after all – though in some cases it would appear that the facts are far stranger than the fiction! In the case of each urban legend I've attempted to present the myth and then explain the facts behind it.

So, the next time someone comes up to you and begins a story with the lines, 'Did you hear about the …' I recommend you take it with a large pinch of salt. But don't forget to throw the salt over your left shoulder afterwards, just in case the Devil is loitering there …

Neil Arnold, 2013

Neil Arnold is a full-time monster-hunter, folklorist, author and lecturer. He has written numerous books, including: *Haunted Rochester*; *Haunted Ashford*; *Haunted Maidstone*; *Haunted Chatham*; *Mystery Animals of the British Isles: Kent*; *Monster!: The A-Z Of Zooform Phenomena*; *Mystery Animals of the British Isles: London*; *Paranormal Kent;* and *Shadows in the Sky: The Haunted Airways of Britain.*

1 BLOODY MARY

> *… the story exists for one reason and one reason alone:*
> *to scare the s**t out of the little kids after the sun goes down.*
>
> ✦
>
> *Danse Macabre,* Stephen King

AS A YOUNGSTER I attended Oaklands Primary School in Walderslade, Chatham. I loved school, and eventually, thanks to some great teachers and their advice over the years, I eventually became a full-time writer. Whilst at school many urban legends were passed around, and quite a few of those I will share with you in this book. One of the first urban legends I heard about was that pertaining to Bloody Mary. A friend of mine told it as follows – in hysterical tone:

> If you go home tonight and go into the bathroom, turn the light out and stare into the mirror whilst holding a candle and say Bloody Mary three times, the ghost of a horrible woman will appear over your shoulder and stay there forever.

This legend freaked me out as a kid, and whilst it may seem an incredibly short ghost story, I'm amazed at how, many decades later, this legend is still repeated in schools throughout the country and across the world. Of course, like many urban myths the Bloody Mary legend can be told in many ways, depending on the storyteller or location. It is popular in American culture too. In some versions the name of Bloody Mary must be said/chanted/whispered three times, in other cases five, whilst others state thirteen because the number thirteen is said to be unlucky. Saying the name of this sinister figure apparently invokes a malignant apparition.

In another version, one must say the Lord's Prayer backwards whilst holding a candle. In yet another, one must carry out this invocation at midnight – if you're brave enough, and as long as your mum and dad don't hear you and give you a scolding for not being in bed! Other variations on the theme state that whilst chanting the name you must run water, spin around several times, rub your eyes, or chant, 'Bloody Mary, I killed your baby.'

Although the Bloody Mary legend is creepy, what I find most amazing is that I've rarely heard anyone question who 'Bloody Mary' is, and I am also confused as to why any frightened child would carry out such a ritual. The legend, of course, exists as a dare, and this theme runs throughout many an urban myth. As in the case of The Hook, it's often about bravery. Courting couples (especially the muscle-bound, macho guy) dismiss the rumour of the hook-handed lunatic for a night of fun in the backseat of a car, but, in the back of their minds, there is always the presence of the shadowy figure – the bogeyman. Are they bold enough to overlook the bogeyman for the sake of passion? In the case of Bloody Mary, I don't recall if I was brave enough as a seven year old to clamber upstairs to the bathroom, turn the light out (find a candle) and then chant the name of some witch-like hag. Those at school who did allegedly do so would then come into school the next day and boast about the fact that nothing weird happened.

Of course, no amount of chanting into a mirror at night could actually conjure up such a demonic entity, but the fear factor was always there. I do recall performing the chant with a couple of mates as a child; nothing happened – thank goodness – but the legend certainly had a power over us as we spurred each other on. Goodness knows what would have happened if a shadowy spectre had appeared in the mirror!

In America, Bloody Mary is believed to have its origins in New Hampshire and allegedly dates back to 1666. The character known as Mary was said to be an orphan who held the town of Portsmouth in fear by stating that fictional horrors would become reality if anyone dared to look into a mirror for long enough. It's possible that Mary was accused of being a witch, and several angry locals hunted her down only to find her dead, her eyes gouged from their sockets. Another tenuous explanation is that the phantom figure is Queen Mary I, who was known as Bloody Mary by her Protestant political opponents during her reign from 1553 until her death in 1558. Twelve-year-old Charlie Ford confirmed to me that this legend was being told when he attended Cuxton Junior School. In his version, those brave enough had to spin around ten times in front of the mirror, then say 'Scary Mary' three times to conjure the spectre, who would jump out of the mirror.

As a child, the actual background details of the Bloody Mary ritual mattered not, because the brief legend seemed horrifying enough. Bloody Mary preyed on our innocent and naïve minds, and for me stirred up all sorts of satanic imagery that, until that time, I had no knowledge of. Another friend told me that at his school in Gillingham, back in the early 1980s, it was rumoured that Bloody Mary could be evoked if you stood in darkness, staring into a mirror whilst holding a flickering candle, saying a certain rhyme backwards. He couldn't remember the rhyme, he said, because he was never brave enough to say it. Interestingly, the Bloody Mary myth also circulated among the female pupils, but their version, which was equally morbid, differed slightly. It was said that young women could find out who they were to marry if, on a dark night, they ascended the stairs of their house – backwards – holding a candle and a small mirror. At some point the face of their future husband would flit into view in the mirror – all well and good. But the hideous side of the legend was that if a horrible skull, or the hooded head of the Grim Reaper, appeared in the mirror, then you would die before marriage. Oh for the joys of childhood! There is an alternative ritual that young girls can conduct to find out their prospective husband. It is said that all one needs is an apple and a secluded spot. The young woman should then utter:

Apple peel, apple peel twist then rest,
Show me the one that I'll love best,
Apple peel over my shoulder fly
Show me the one I'll love till I die

And with that the peel should be cast over the shoulder and, after hitting the ground, will resemble a letter of the alphabet – thought to be the first letter of the future husband's name.

There is a possibility that these mirror legends stem from catoptromancy, a form of divination carried out using a mirror. A Greek traveller named Pausanias recorded a similar legend to Bloody Mary as early as the second century AD:

Before the Temple of Ceres at Patras, there was a fountain, separated from the temple by a wall, and there was an oracle, very truthful, not for all events, but for the sick only. The sick person let down a mirror, suspended by a thread till its base touched the surface of the water, having first prayed to the goddess and offered incense. Then looking in the mirror, he saw the presage of death or recovery, according as the face appeared fresh and healthy, or of ghastly aspect.

It may also be worth quoting the classic 'Mirror mirror on the wall, who is the fairest of them all?' from the fairy tale *Snow White*. The magic mirror appears in the German version of the tale collected by the Brothers Grimm in 1812. Stories such as Oscar Wilde's *The Picture of Dorian Gray*, Lewis Carroll's *Through the Looking Glass* and Tennyson's poem *The Lady of Shalott*, also refer to the mirror as having spiritual properties.

When I was young I was often told that mirrors were a portal to an ethereal void – a place where spirits could enter and exit. I was of the belief that items, or even people, could be pulled into mirrors, and that by staring into a mirror one could view the scene in a completely different light – and maybe see things which weren't actually there. And this is why the legend of Bloody Mary is powerful, because by staring constantly into a mirror there is an air of unreality about it, especially when the room is dark except for a flickering candle.

I'll leave you with a modern interpretation of the Bloody Mary legend which goes by various names, ranging from the Midnight Man to the Shadow Man. Nowadays it seems that kids are more eager to experiment with legends, rather than just stand in front of a mirror. In the case of the Midnight Man, you will need (just like on *Blue Peter*!) a pencil, a piece of paper, a door in the house, salt, a candle, matches, a ticking clock and a needle. You must then turn off the lights, light the candle and write your name – Christian name first, then any middle names, then your surname – on the piece of paper. Then, if you're brave enough, prick your finger with the needle and splash a drop of crimson onto your written name and allow the blood to soak in. After this, place the bit of blood-caked paper in front of the door. Then, on the stroke of midnight, knock on the door (coinciding with the ticking of the clock) as many times as the legend suggests – some say thirteen times, others twenty-two – then open the door, blow out the candle, and then close the door; according to the legend, you have now summoned the Midnight/Shadow Man. It's then best to relight your candle – if you can find the matches in the dark! – and, for the next goodness knows how long, you must attempt to avoid the Midnight Man. You'll know he is near because the candle will go out, followed by strange whispering and a rush of cold air, and at that point the sinister demon will appear in front of you. It is your job to relight the candle within ten seconds. If you fail to do so, you must grab the salt, draw a circle around yourself, and stay in the circle from 12.01 a.m. until 3.33 a.m. Hopefully, you'll still be alive by then but, if you fail, then you die.

Personally, I'd love to know what happens when the Midnight Man bumps into Bloody Mary on a dark and stormy night. And with that, it seems fitting to leave you with an excerpt from Thomas Ingoldsby's book, *The Ingoldsby Legends*, which I recommend you read in front of a mirror, whilst holding a candle!

> He drew the mystic circle's bound,
> With skull and cross-bones fenc'd around;
> He traced full many a sigil there;
> He mutter'd many a backward pray'r …

THE PHANTOM
HITCH-HIKER

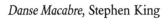

*It's what the mind sees that makes these stories
such quintessential tales of terror.*

◆

Danse Macabre, **Stephen King**

IF THERE'S ONE urban legend that changed my life it is that of The Phantom Hitch-hiker. This vehicle-related myth remains one of the creepiest urban legends I have ever come across, and was told to me when I was around eight or nine years of age. I was fortunate enough to grow up in a loving family whose stories of ghosts and monsters inspired me to become a monster-hunter and author of books pertaining to folklore and mystery. As a child, growing up in Walderslade, I lived very close to a purportedly haunted location – a small, yet very old, village known as Blue Bell Hill. The village, situated a few miles short of the town of Maidstone, is in fact a large chalk hill. The village is divided – due to the construction of a dual carriageway in the 1970s – into two parts, the Upper Bell and the Lower Bell. A beautiful picnic area sits atop the Upper Bell and provides a panoramic view across the North Downs, and at the bottom of the hill – known as the Lower Bell – runs the ancient trackway known as the Pilgrims' Way.

The village of Blue Bell Hill is steeped in history, which in turns brings folklore, and the lore and legends of the hill are rife. As a child, my dad told me a terrifying story pertaining to Blue Bell Hill and it is a story that has never left me. Even through maturity it maintained its chill. It was told to me one dark night when my dad took me to the Chatham Road, which runs from the Lower Bell public house to the A229 dual carriageway. Now, I'll try to set the scene, so come with me …

✳ ✳ ✳

My dad and granddad always told me ghost stories, and the most common yarn passed around and down through families in Medway back in the early 1980s was the tale of the phantom hitch-hiker of Blue Bell Hill. It begins on a rain-soaked winter evening, close to midnight, where we meet a lone motorist travelling within the vicinity of Blue Bell Hill. According to the legend, this chap is driving towards the Chatham Road – thunder is reverberating around the sky, lightning forks spear down from the heavens, and the windscreen wipers of the man's car are working overtime to combat the downpour. As he crosses over a junction near the Lower Bell pub, and heads up the Chatham Road, he notices, standing by the side of the road on the left, a young woman. The lady is wearing a whitish, flimsy dress, her hair is matted due to the bad weather, and she looks rather out of place standing on the verge in the torrential rain. Now, Blue Bell Hill, especially the lower part of the village, is not heavily populated. The area is wooded, and apart from the pub and a nearby cottage, there are no houses to directly speak of, and so the driver wonders to himself why on earth a young woman is out at such a late hour, in such weather, and wearing what seems to be inappropriate clothing for that time of year. So, the man decides he'll pull over by the side of the road and offer a lift to the rain-soaked woman. The woman slips into the backseat of the vehicle (in some cases she gets into the passenger seat) and asks to be taken to a destination somewhere within a few miles of Blue Bell Hill. This detail also varies, depending on the storyteller.

The man pulls away from the side of the road. He tries to have a conversation with the drenched woman, but the legend states that little or no words are exchanged. However, when the man reaches the dual carriageway, he either a) looks into his rear-view mirror, or b) turns round briefly to talk to the woman in white, but she has, to his astonishment, completely vanished. Now, according to my father's version of the eerie events, this driver does not believe in ghosts but can't think where this young woman has gone, and so he decides to drive to the house to enquire about the girl. In another version of the urban legend, the girl is said to leave behind a coat, purse, handbag or sweater, which the man decides to bring to the house where she had asked to be taken.

By the time the man reaches the house it has gone midnight and the rain is still beating down hard on the tarmac. He pulls up outside the house, gets out of his car and walks up the gravel drive. He knocks on the door and, after a short wait, a light comes on inside the house. The door opens a fraction – obviously the people who live there are hesitant to open the door to anyone at such a time of night – and they ask him what he wants. The man tells the couple (who are usually said to be between fifty and seventy) that he picked up a girl in white on Blue Bell Hill but she vanished from the backseat. In another version, he hands over the coat/purse/handbag/sweater that the woman left behind. After describing the girl to the couple he is told, to his utmost horror, that the girl is in fact their daughter but she died several years ago! Another storyteller of this urban legend may mention that the elderly couple say, 'This happens all the time.' Whatever the case, it is not only a creepy ghost story but one of the most classic urban legends.

∗ ∗ ∗

If you trawl the Internet, or pick up any one of the countless ghost-related books from all over the world, you are likely to find a story pertaining to a phantom hitch-hiker. If you are a believer in ghosts then you might assume that road ghosts are quite common, especially when you consider the number of fatalities which occur on roads each year; however, The Phantom Hitch-hiker legend is very different. When I first heard this story, within the setting of that old hill, I truly believed that a woman in white must loiter around the area. It was the perfect place for a ghost story. As it was my dad who had told me this story, and as he had also claimed that he knew someone who knew someone that this had happened to, I was completely hooked – without realising that I was simply part of a chain and that shortly afterwards I would tell many school friends about the phantom hitch-hiker of Blue Bell Hill.

Living so close to Blue Bell Hill meant that this story wasn't far removed from me, and so I decided, as a curious child, to investigate this fascinating case. I spoke to relatives – uncles and cousins who'd all apparently known someone who had picked up that girl – but the amazing thing was, I never, not once, spoke to someone who had actually picked that woman up. The phantom hitch-hiker of Blue Bell Hill was the first urban legend I was ever introduced to and, for me, it's still the best. Weirdly, as I got older, more and more people entered my life who claimed to have known someone who knew someone else who had picked up that girl; details were always vague except for the fact – or alleged facts – that a) the girl wore white (possibly a bridal or bridesmaid's dress), b) it happened on a sopping autumnal/winter night, and c) it occurred around the late 1960s or early '70s. Usually the witness failed to remember where the girl had asked to be dropped off, but in some cases the story would alter and witnesses claimed they had dropped the girl somewhere near either Maidstone or Chatham, but she had vanished once out of the car.

The phantom hitch-hiker of Blue Bell Hill is echoed around the world. In Chicago, America, there is a hitch-hiker ghost known as Resurrection Mary. It is claimed that this legend dates back to the 1930s when people, usually young men, reported picking up a woman on Archer Avenue. The woman is said to wear a whitish party dress, and has blonde hair and blue eyes. As in the case of the Blue Bell Hill ghost, Resurrection Mary is said to hold a bag or purse, and whilst in the vehicle she says very little except that she wants to be dropped off outside Resurrection Cemetery. The driver obliges but the young woman vanishes as she enters the cemetery. Allegedly, many years ago, a woman on her way to a party was the victim of a fatal hit-and-run, and now she forever haunts the area, possibly searching for the person who took her life.

Another hitch-hiker case centres upon the Nunney to Frome road in Somerset, in the South West of England. Since the 1970s, drivers have reported picking up or hitting a spectre on this stretch of road. The reputedly haunted village of Pluckley in Kent also has its own ghostly hitch-hiker. A few years ago, taxi driver Raymond Breakspear claimed to have picked up an unexpected fare at around 2.45 a.m. According to Raymond, who spoke about his encounter on the television programme *Strange But True?*, the man slipped into the backseat of the taxi but when Raymond turned to ask the man where he wanted to go, there was no sign of the mystery passenger.

A surreal phantom hitch-hiker encounter took place a few years ago in Dothan, Israel. A resident of Jenin was heading towards Dothan one night when he stopped to pick up a female hitch-hiker. The woman climbed into the passenger seat, but when the driver turned to speak to the woman, her face had transformed into that of a one-eyed dog. In other cases, drivers have reported that the female hitch-hiker has the legs of a goat and warns them of the coming of the Messiah! In *Haunted Ashford* I spoke of another extraordinary ghostly hitch-hiker experienced by a lady named Gina McCartney. In 1984, Gina was driving through Great Chart one night when she looked in her rear-view mirror and saw someone sit up in the backseat. Commenting to the *Evening Post* of 21 November 1984, Gina stated that the phantom passenger appeared to be a man aged between thirty and thirty-five. When Gina looked back again there was no one in the backseat, but as soon as she faced the dark road again the engine of the vehicle cut out. Gina tried starting the engine but to no avail, so she got out of the car and noticed that she had a flat tyre. She went to the boot to get a jack, but when she returned the tyre was no longer flat. Gina hurriedly got back into the car, turned the key, and it started first time. She drove home to her husband, and, rather shaken, told him of her frightful encounter.

Sceptics among you may argue that ghosts do not exist and that witnesses to the so-called phantom hitch-hiker may well have been part of a hoax, or else were simply tired and prone to hallucination. However, due to the amount of cases worldwide, it would seem that the urban legend is much more than just a figment of the imagination, and Kent seems to be a particular hotbed for such activity. There are numerous cases on record from towns such as Tunbridge Wells, Gillingham, Tenterden and Sevenoaks, where people claim to have either hit spectral jaywalkers or picked up a hitch-hiker who then disappears. As in the case of Chicago's Resurrection Mary, there appears to be some documented background to the legend of the Blue Bell Hill ghost. In November 1965, a terrible crash involving two vehicles took place at Blue Bell Hill, which resulted in the death of three young women. One of these women was a bride-to-be, due to be married the following day. She died five days after the crash due to the severity of her injuries. Her friends in the car were to be bridesmaids. Eerily, such a tragic crash brings to mind the urban legend known as the Vanishing Bridesmaids, which originates from Great Melton in Norfolk, where it is said that a spectral coach, harbouring four bridesmaids, is seen along a certain stretch of road. The legend states that the girls were returning late from a wedding when they, and the coach they were travelling in, simply vanished into thin air – as if they'd slipped through a tear in the fabric of time.

It seems that ever since the 1965 crash, people have jumped to the conclusion that the phantom hitch-hiker of the hill must surely be her, or maybe one of her bridesmaids. It makes for an almost romantic story, which has been passed down through several generations. Maybe, just maybe, there have been a few sporadic sightings of a girl in a whitish dress on the hill, and one can see why families, and even newspaper reporters, love this tale of a ghostly bride-to-be lurking on that foggy hill. Maybe she still waits for the sweetheart she never got to marry. According to some, she hitches a lift hoping to get to the church on time. Others go for a more sinister version of events and claim that she remains lost on the hill, hoping to find those who accidentally took her life. It all makes for a spooky treat indeed, fodder for any Halloween party or crackling campfire; and amazingly, despite being based on a factual crash, the tale echoes countless other phantom hitch-hiker stories from across the world.

During the early 1990s, two frightening incidents took place on Blue Bell Hill. 'Ghost Girl Seen Again' was the front-page headline of the *Kent Today* of 10 November 1992, after fifty-four-year-old coach driver Ian Sharpe claimed to have knocked down a ghostly woman on 8 November in the vicinity of the Aylesford turn-off of the A229. Mr Sharpe, a very level-headed individual, was travelling home to Maidstone when a young lady ran out in front of his vehicle. Ian skidded to a halt and clambered out of his car, but could find no trace of the woman in the undergrowth and so went to the local police station to report what had happened. Despite further investigation, they could not find a body.

Two weeks later a man named Chris Dawkins had a very similar encounter, but this time further up the hill near the Robin Hood Lane junction. At 10.55 p.m., on 22 November 1992, Mr Dawkins was travelling home when a woman ran out in front of his Toyota car and went under the vehicle. He searched the area but could find no trace of her and so phoned his dad from a nearby telephone box. When his father arrived on the scene, Chris broke down in tears, very distressed by the event. Police were phoned from a nearby house but, after much searching, they also failed to find any sign of the young woman Chris had described hitting.

In these cases the so-called ghost did not hitch a lift and vanish from the vehicle interior. However, it seems that witnesses did indeed have a spectral encounter, and this type of incident has been reported from Blue Bell Hill on numerous occasions. One of the best known involves a chap named Maurice Goodenough who, in the early hours of

13 July 1974, reported to Rochester police station that he'd hit a young girl – aged approximately ten – on Blue Bell Hill. On this occasion, when the motorist got out of his vehicle, the girl was lying in the road and appeared very real. According to the shocked witness, the girl was wearing a white blouse, a skirt and white ankle socks, and had shoulder-length brown hair. Mr Goodenough attempted to flag down some passing cars but with no success, and so decided to leave the girl by the roadside and drive to the local police station. When he returned with the police around thirty minutes later, aided by a tracker dog, there was no sign of the little girl. At the time, the conclusion of the press was that the girl, due to her disappearance from the scene, must have been a ghost – another eerie tale to add to the already burgeoning spooky reputation of the hill.

Whilst there are many stories regarding a hitchhiking ghostly bride-to-be, the majority of the cases on the hill are nothing of the sort. Have genuine encounters in fact taken place? Just what is going on? I've given many lectures across the South East of England pertaining to folklore, and when I mention Blue Bell Hill I'm amazed at the number of people in the audience who come forward to report that they knew of someone who had picked up a girl around the area. Usually, they tell the story of how the girl is a ghostly bride-to-be who died in a car accident. What most people – especially those who are part of the chain – do not realise, is that this is by no means the hill's only story.

In 1934, a man riding a motorbike with a sidecar claimed to have picked up a young woman on the hill. She asked to be taken to Church Street at the neighbouring village of Burham, but vanished upon reaching her destination. In another incident in the late 1960s, or possibly early '70s, two men claimed they'd picked up a young woman at Blue Bell Hill who then vanished near Rochester Airport.

In October 1968, Joe Chester was pushing his bicycle up the slip road which runs next to the now-derelict Upper Bell public house when a woman, damp with rain and wearing a light flowery dress, walked out in front of him. The woman veered away from Joe (maybe she realised she couldn't get knocked down by a man pushing a bike!) and vanished. On another occasion, a couple driving at Blue Bell Hill in the mid-1990s claimed to have seen a 'bridesmaid' standing in the undergrowth; whilst in the 1970s another couple claimed to have seen a ghostly woman wearing 'old-fashioned clothing' walking along the Chatham Road. The woman had vanished by the time the couple looked back.

Are the encounters with a ghostly girl all part of some vast, complex legend that has somehow over the years come to life as people travel, mainly at night, up Blue Bell Hill? I've spent many days and nights up Blue Bell Hill but have never seen a phantom – although I do recall a few years ago seeing a local man on the hill at night dressed up as a woman! As cars travelled up the Chatham Road he would jump out to startle them. Rather dangerous, one would imagine, but even so, it all adds to the strange folklore of the place.

In his fascinating work *The Vanishing Hitch-hiker*, author Jan Harold Brunvand writes of many American urban legends, including road spooks dating back to the early 1900s. In most cases, the witnesses – or at least people who claim to know the witnesses – state they've picked up a man or woman who vanishes from the backseat of the car. A slight variation on the female hitch-hiker story is that a man and his friend get chatting to a woman in a bar, who coincidentally lives in their neighbourhood. She asks them if they will take her home and they comply. The men get into the front of the car, the woman slips into the back, and they head off into the night. According to the storyteller, it is such a cold night that the woman asks one of the men if she can borrow his coat, and the man obliges. However, as they reach the local cemetery the woman suddenly asks the driver if he can stop to let her out. The men are rather bemused by this but stop the car, and the woman tells them to wait. But after quite a few minutes she does not return. The urban legend reaches its climax when the men, rather annoyed by the woman's disappearance – and the fact that she is still wearing the coat – get out of the car and investigate the cemetery. After a few minutes the men come to a grave and the coat is draped on the headstone. The grave belongs to the girl they picked up. Whoa!

Of course, this makes for atmospheric reading, but how can we sort out the allegedly real encounters from the urban legend? Well, it's nigh on impossible to do so because, no matter how seemingly genuine the encounters, ghosts are never likely to be scientifically proven, and so every incident simply adds to the legend – which must be frustrating for those adamant that they've had a terrifying encounter with a ghost. The 1934 encounter involving the man on a motorbike perhaps bears some resemblance to the Resurrection Mary legend, as the area he dropped the woman off was near an old churchyard – so to an extent there appears to be a crossover between fact and legend. Researcher Sean Tudor notes how, despite being of a bizarre nature, most cases are 'enacted in accordance to a fairly strict pattern'. He comments that in most of the stories the witness is a lone male who sees a ghostly female – often wearing white or light clothing. Sean also notes the 'very similar behaviour [of stepping deliberately into, or waiting in the path of, an oncoming vehicle], giving the motorist no opportunity to avoid a collision', and states that most incidents occur between 11 p.m. and 1 a.m. Sean further mentions that the ghost is rarely caught in the act of disappearing, and says that many of these urban legends revolve around an anniversary, usually of a tragic death. Together, these factors form an 'idealized phantom hitch-hiker script'. In fact, the only difference between The Phantom Hitch-hiker legend and the ghostly road collision seems to be that the hitch-hiker is very much an anecdote, passed around as Chinese whispers, whereas the collisions are reported to the press first-hand, as if they actually took place. In several cases of ghostly collisions, police have been called out to investigate the missing body.

It could be argued, then, that The Phantom Hitch-hiker legend is nothing more than a story created around a campfire, which somehow, over the decades, has taken on a life of its own. I've always been of the opinion that if you believe in something enough it can start to happen. Press influence, whispers and rumour all add to the melting pot, and you can guarantee that somewhere out there there's someone who knows someone who has experienced something to fit in with that current urban legend. As aforementioned, urban legends can create hysteria, panic, and many other emotions, if we believe in them enough. And yet we can't simply discard so many stories as fiction can we?

In his book, Brunvand mentions an intriguing tale from New York, dating back to the late 1800s, pertaining to a woman who had heard of a female ghost who, on certain nights, would attach herself to a horse and rider as they galloped by. The phantom would only disappear once the rider had reached his destination. I have found a similar

Kentish legend mentioned by chronicler Charles Igglesden in *A Saunter through Kent with Pen and Pencil*. He speaks of a phantom hitch-hiker in the village of Benenden, in the Tunbridge Wells district. Many years ago, a man named Hunt was due to marry a lady named Peggy, but Mr Hunt was not to be trusted for, over the years, and whilst with Peggy, he had had a string of affairs. On the day Hunt was due to marry Peggy, the unfortunate bride-to-be arrived at the church only to find that her future husband had already married her sister! Peggy was said, in a forlorn state, to have drowned herself in the local pond. One night, however, while riding home on his cart, Hunt was joined by the ghost of Peggy, who climbed aboard his wagon and remained there until they reached the stables – and then completely vanished. The encounter left Hunt in a terrible state.

Again, we find a familiar set of details – the bride-to-be who never got wed, and the loveless ghost girl hitching a lift and then vanishing at a certain point of the journey, leaving the witness terror-stricken. Brunvand mentions how, over the years, the New York story took on several twists and that there is a similar tale, stemming from Arkansas in the 1940s, which involves a phantom hitch-hiker named Lucy. This ghost appears behind the male motorcyclist, clinging to him tightly and breathing down his neck; she asks to be dropped off near a remote churchyard.

Of course, usually we look for a reason why there's a ghost roaming town, and, whilst in most cases we create our own origins, in the case of Blue Bell Hill we have an actual crash, and as you'll read a possible murder, to add credence to our story. The 1934 incident involving the man on the motorbike dates back several decades before the 1965 crash on the hill. However, the murder which could have spawned this urban legend took place in 1916. A young lady named Emily Trigg, who worked as a servant girl in Rochester, lived at Blue Bell Hill – not far, coincidentally, from Chris Dawkins' encounter. After work she would walk home and pass an area known as Bridge Wood, a site now occupied by the Bridgewood Hotel at Walderslade. It was near here that Emily's body was found a short while after she was killed, so maybe it is her ghost that roams Blue Bell Hill. Of course, when this is explained, many people ask why she would ask for a lift to the churchyard in Burham – but the tale is made even spookier when the storyteller reveals that this is the churchyard where Miss Trigg is buried. So, once again, there are a number of actual facts we can use to bolster a ghostly urban legend. In the case of Emily Trigg, we are accounting for the ghostly sightings which occurred prior to the 1965 crash.

We also find rumour that in the early 1940s a young woman was run over on Blue Bell Hill. The unnamed woman was, apparently, cycling to meet her boyfriend in the vicinity of Rochester Airport. Whilst riding through Blue Bell Hill village, her bicycle chain became loose; the young lady hopped off her bike to tend to the chain but struggled to reattach it, and so decided to flag down a passing lorry. Sadly, as she ran out in front of the vehicle with arms flailing, the side of the lorry glanced her, causing her to spin and lose her footing, and she fell under the back wheels. Perhaps this is why the Blue Bell Hill ghost runs out in front of vehicles.

The *Evening Post* of 12 August 1969 mentions that a road ghost was seen in the area 'at the turn of the century'. According to the paper, '… a group of Chatham youths went to the Upper Bell public house for an evening out. While drinking they discussed the idea of laying the phantom of the nearby Common Road in Burham'. On this occasion, however, the road spectre was far from being a woman in white. 'The ghost they had in mind was a one-eyed phantom that passes quickly along the road in the night.' The young men were keen to catch a glimpse of the wraith, but whilst in the pub another youth overheard the men and decided to play a prank. Dressing in a white sheet, holding a lit cigar (to act as the glowing eye) and riding a bike in the dark seemed to be the best way to appear as the one-eyed phantom. The hoaxer cycled by the ghost-hunters – but one of them heard the bike and picked up the smell of tobacco. Sensing that something odd was afoot, when the 'ghost' came back they accosted it, giving the prankster quite a beating.

Maybe Blue Bell Hill does harbour several ghosts. It's one of those places. And over the years a few people have certainly died whilst travelling on the busy stretch of dual carriageway. But the location, like Resurrection Cemetery, seems to be a hotbed of weird activity, rather than just a place where ghostly encounters take place once every blue moon. A few eyewitnesses have even come forward to report sightings of an old hag, mainly from the stretch of road known as the Old Chatham Road, which runs alongside the Chatham Road. This is a different type of manifestation, that has no interest in getting into a car or being knocked down by one. Instead, the entity appears as a seemingly malevolent, shabby spectre that accosts vehicles! In some cases the figure gives a dire warning, and certainly seems to be a bad omen. Many years ago, two men were driving along a country road in Kent late at night when they saw, standing by the side of the road, an old woman. The men decided to ask the woman – who was in the middle of nowhere – if she wanted a lift, to which she replied in sinister fashion, 'Don't you ever cross my path again,' and shook her fist at them. She may simply have been a flesh-and-blood woman angered by the men's intrusion on her nightly stroll, but her reaction never left their minds.

Another legend comes from a man named Tom Atkinson, a Maidstone resident who recalls a frightful legend told to him by school friends. They claimed that a witch-like figure haunted Blue Bell Hill accompanied by a phantom hound or two, which she would let off their leashes, enabling them to scamper in front of vehicles. A different version states that the woman rides an old cart and directs people up the hill to safety.

Several people have come forward over the years to speak of their encounters with a woman in black on the old hill. The most recent incident involved a female motorist named Beth Hayes, who was driving home from work one November evening in 2010. She had come off the dual carriageway at the Aylesford turn off and was heading toward the Lower Bell public house, which is on the left, when she noticed a figure dressed in a long black trench coat standing by the side of the road. Beth was busy concentrating on the road but could see the coat flapping in the wind and she was concerned that the figure was going to step out in front of her. But as she drove by, the figure vanished. Oddly, there was nowhere for it to have gone in such a short space of time. Had Beth seen the old hag? We'll never know, but legend has it that the woman in black frequents the hill on autumn nights.

All around the world, people pass down the following legend: someone they know once picked up a young, beautiful woman who, halfway through the journey, went through a weird metamorphosis, changing into an old woman – or, as in the case of the Israel hitch-hiker, a half-human, half-monster wraith. This malevolent version of The Phantom Hitch-hiker legend almost crosses over into another popular urban myth, one which brings to mind the aforementioned Gina McCartney incident at Great Chart, but on a more sinister level. The Killer in the Backseat is classic campfire stuff, and goes something like this:

A young woman drives to a friend's house in a remote location. After having a nice meal and pleasant chat she decides it's time to go home as it's getting late. She gets in the car, bids farewell to her friend, and heads off under the cloak of night. As she pulls away from the drive she notices another car start up behind her. A few minutes into her journey, and on a dark stretch of road, she notices that the other car is still behind her, and gaining ground. Unnervingly, the car behind seems to pull up close, to within a few feet of her rear bumper, and yet despite her attempts to let the car pass it never does. By this time the woman is extremely uneasy, spooked by the presence of the car which is now beginning to flash its headlights, almost blinding her in the rear-view mirror. The woman now speeds up, eager to get home, and on two occasions drives straight through a red light – only to see her pursuer do the same. It has gone midnight by the time she gets home and swings into her driveway; and she scrambles out of the car in time to see the mysterious vehicle pull in right behind her. The woman has had enough of the intimidation and so decides to confront the driver – or, in some versions, she pulls into the drive and sounds her horn, waking her husband, who comes rushing down the stairs to her aid. Either way, the driver of the other car is confronted. The terrified yet brave woman yells at the man, asking him what his problem is. The classic story is that the woman's husband then grabs the man in the other car, pulls him out into the street, and is about to give him a beating … when the mystery pursuer barks, 'I followed your wife because as

I got into my car and turned my headlights on, I noticed a man's head ducked down in her backseat.'

With that, the husband rushes to look at the backseat of the car and there, hunched down, is a man holding an axe!

According to Jan Harold Van Brunvand, this urban legend first appeared in Utah in 1968, and yet I've heard this told in Kent. I recall a case from Canterbury several years ago, maybe from the early 1990s, passed down through a friend of a friend. One night, whilst driving home from university, this person realised they were being followed by another car, which was flashing its headlights and beeping its horn loudly. Without knowing it, they were actually being warned by the other vehicle that there was someone in the backseat holding an axe or knife, depending on who you hear this tale from. Of course the details, once again, are extremely vague; the location is always so remote that the storyteller can't quite put their finger on where or when it took place.

The Killer in the Backseat certainly has echoes of The Phantom Hitch-hiker in the sense that we are dealing with an unsettling intruder. It also brings to mind the case of The Boyfriend's Death (*see* Introduction). These automobile-related legends remind us to always check our vehicles for unwanted passengers! Brunvand mentions another possible variant, in that the killer is on top of the vehicle, hanging from the roof rack. In this version, the driver is told by an observer to swerve the car across the road; of course, the motorist doesn't understand why and thinks this is crazy – until the killer comes flying off the roof and hits the ground. In another version, the victim pulls into a petrol station late at night on a remote stretch, but when the driver – in this case nearly always a lone woman – attempts to pay for the petrol, she is told by the attendant that the money is counterfeit. She begins to suspect that something weird is going on and worries that the member of staff is a little odd and wants to harm her. But the truth is that the attendant is trying to distract her, so he can phone the police to tell them there's a man in the backseat of her car. The setting also reminds us of The Hook, with the twist that the person suspected of being the bogeyman is actually trying to warn us, and the real bogeyman is far closer to home – in the back seat of the car, or leaving his artificial limb dangling from the car door.

Many urban legends appear to be confined to the foggy past, but that is not always the case. In January 2000, a motorist named Keith Scales had a peculiar encounter at Wye, Ashford. Whilst driving through a wooded area known as White Hill at 6.45 a.m., Mr Scales rounded a bend and noticed a woman standing in the road ahead. The driver couldn't stop his vehicle in time and, when he hit the woman, she rolled over his bonnet. When Mr Scales got out of his car to investigate, he could find no trace of the woman. Ring any bells? However, what makes this peculiar encounter different is the fact that the spectre had caused some sort of damage to the car – the wing mirror on the right-hand side had been cracked. Mr John Rogers, a former chairman of Wye Parish Council, remarked that Mr Scales had probably hit a white deer, even though the startled motorist stated quite categorically that the figure he had hit was a woman with long blonde hair and wearing a long, dark coat.

Interestingly, there is another phantom hitch-hiker legend from Wye. It concerns a male driver who, a few years ago, offered a young woman a lift outside Wye railway station as she had missed the last train. The woman asked to be taken somewhere in Ashford. The next day, the unnerved motorist reported to the local railway attendant that the woman he had picked up had had no face when he turned to speak to her.

In another strange case, from 1988, police were called out to the A2 near Bowaters, at Gillingham, after the sighting of a 'weird figure'. Now, let me digress for a moment – in America, there is an urban legend which concerns a lone driver who is travelling along a stretch of road at night when suddenly a car appears up ahead with no headlights on. The urban legend states that if the unsuspecting driver flashes their lights at the approaching vehicle, they will be killed. Basically, the people driving the car with the headlights off are gang members initiating someone into their group. The first vehicle to flash its lights at them will be accosted. So, what has this got to do with the A2 'weird figure'? Well, the report at the time – from the *Chatham Standard* – mentions that the motorist told police he'd seen an apparition which had a 'white painted face and seemed to be floating along the central reservation'. The witness also reported that the scene seemed to be triggered by a parked car that was flashing its headlights on and off. According to the paper, 'Police found no trace of the ghost but believed that the witness was genuine.' The fact that there was a car parked nearby suggests some type of hoax – but the pranksters were careful not to get run over, by keeping their 'spook' on the central reservation rather than straying into the road!

The Phantom Hitch-hiker is one of Kent's best-known urban legends, and I'm pretty sure that whatever phenomena plague Blue Bell Hill, and other sites around the county for that matter, the oft-mentioned myth concerning the girl disappearing from the backseat will always exist, even if no one actually picks her up. On a more comical note, another vehicle-related urban legend, known as the Abducted Mechanic, has done the rounds in Kent.

In this urban legend, a member of the public makes a report to the police after seeing a child being locked into the boot of a car which then drove off. When the police set off in hot pursuit and track the car down, they open the boot and find a dwarf. However, the short guy is in fact a mechanic, and the reason he's in the boot of the car is because the driver had just brought the car into the garage due to an annoying rattle in the boot. The mechanic had then asked the driver if he could lie in the boot whilst the owner drove around, in order to find out where the noise was coming from! This story allegedly originated from Germany in 2007, but in the Kentish town of Dover a very similar incident took place in 1977 and may have been responsible for spawning this quirky automobile-related legend. According to sources, and in some cases rumour, during March 1977 Dover police were contacted by a hysterical woman who stated that she'd seen a car driving extremely fast with a body sticking out of the boot. The woman had taken down the registration number and make of the vehicle and, in a matter of minutes, the police were on the case. As they approached the speeding vehicle, they could see the two legs sticking out the boot, but when they finally managed to flag down the car they were amazed to find that the 'body' was in fact a mechanic who had been listening for a pesky rattle! There's another, more disturbing, mechanic-related urban legend which has done the rounds through the world too, and concerns – once again – a lone woman. She puts her car into the garage for a service and the strange man who works there asks her to leave her keys; he then takes them to a shop and gets them copied in order to break into her house at night and assault her.

Another sinister legend regarding vehicles comes from the vicinity of Bluewater Shopping Centre, near Greenhithe. The shopping centre attracts thousands of people each year, and so it's no wonder that legends pertaining to the place come about. One such urban legend – which has many similarities to The Killer in the Backseat –centres upon a lone female who drives into the car park at the shopping centre and notices a man, dressed very smartly, peering under the bonnet of his car. The woman pulls up alongside the man and asks if everything is okay; he responds that his car appears to have broken down, which is a major concern as he has a very important appointment. The woman decides, very kindly, to offer the man a lift and he smiles, retrieves his briefcase from his redundant car, and hops into the passenger side. The woman then begins to drive but, after a short while, wonders what the hell she's doing giving a lift to a stranger and starts to panic inwardly. She tells the man that her tyre feels flat and asks him if he wouldn't mind getting out and checking. The man obligingly gets out of the car, and the woman, in fear, drives off. When she is about half a mile away from the man, the woman suddenly realises that his briefcase is in the car, and she feels guilty that she's driven off. She pulls over by the side of the road to check the contents of the briefcase – and to her horror her gaze is met by an assortment of knives, hammers and other grisly tools. The motorist drives to the nearest police station and tells the officer on duty what has happened. After showing him the briefcase, the policeman tells the shaken woman that she's had a lucky escape from the 'car park killer'!

In America there is another version, in which it is an old woman who turns up at a shopping mall begging a lone motorist for a ride. In another account, it is said that a gang of car-jacking thugs are doing the rounds and accost motorists by hiding under a parked vehicle. When the driver – usually a lone female – comes to her car, the gang member slashes at her ankles and Achilles heel with a knife!

The fascinating and modern 'car park killer' legend is clearly an alternative take on The Killer in the Backseat, and I was amazed to find reference to it on a Student Midwife website! Even more intriguing was the fact that after the 'car park killer' story was mentioned and dismissed as legend, someone else contributed with another road-related yarn – which they were sure was real because they'd heard it from their sister-in-law who knew someone it had happened to. The contributor, named Iris, mentioned that her sister-in-law, a newly qualified nurse, had made friends with another newly qualified nurse and both had started their new job on the same day. According to Iris, the hospital they worked in was situated at the end of a remote road, so if the nurses worked on the same shift, they would leave together, following each other out onto the isolated lane for reassurance. It seems that one night the other nurse had been working alone on her shift and drove out onto the isolated road when she spotted something – which looked like a body – lying on the tarmac up ahead. As she approached, she decided to get out of her car for a better look and, to her relief, noticed that the object was simply some strewn rags. The woman then got back into her vehicle and drove away. But a few moments later a car appeared behind her, beeping its horn and flashing its lights; eventually it pulled up alongside her, overtook her and then swerved suddenly in front, blocking her path. The woman in the car was obviously terrified, expecting some lunatic to emerge from the car in front, when suddenly there was a movement in the back seat of her own car. As she looked around she was stunned to see a man sit up, open the door and rush out into the blackness. It seems that the other car had saved her life from The Killer in the Backseat.

Iris concluded her tale by stating, 'Okay, I do not know the woman this happened to but I do know for a fact my sister-in-law knew this woman and was in contact with her for a while afterwards.' Sadly, however believable this seems, the pattern of detail suggests it is nothing more than an urban legend. Even so, at times these legends may become reality for some, especially if there's some unhinged character out there hoping to make fact out of the fiction.

In another alleged case from Kent – Swanley, to be precise – dating back to October 1998, a woman was driving when she was flashed down by a male motorist, who shouted across to her that her tyre was flat. The woman was hesitant to pull over, and so the man in the other car said he would stay close to make sure she got home alright – but instead she drove to a local garage and suddenly the man sped away. This echoes a very sinister case from California in the 1960s when a man – thought to be the serial killer known as 'Zodiac' – reportedly flagged down a woman and her baby, who were driving on a stretch of highway at night. The man told the woman that she had problems with her wheel and said he would fix it, but instead he unscrewed some of the nuts around the tyre. The woman, not realising what he had done, thanked the man and drove off – but the wheel literally fell off. The man pulled up alongside the woman and said it must have been worse than he thought and offered her a lift. Once in his car, the woman became unnerved and the mysterious man seemed to become very agitated at the sight of her baby. He told her he was going to kill her, but bravely she leapt from the vehicle with her baby in her arms.

Police believed the woman had had a very lucky escape from one of America's worst serial killers – a man who had taunted police for several years. He was never caught, and, rather oddly, his antics in the case of the woman and the baby bear strong similarities to urban legend. Again, this tale acts as a scare story and a wake-up call to any lone motorist who is driving along an isolated stretch of road.

In November 2012 the Kent Online website reported: 'A motorist has been trying to get lone women drivers to pull over at night with a fake sign about them having a flat tyre.' Female motorists were put on alert following an incident involving a solitary woman. She claimed that, whilst driving late one night on the A2 from London to Kent, she had been overtaken by another vehicle. Someone in the car had held up a sign saying something along the lines of 'Pull over you've got a flat tyre'. The report added: 'She did not pull over until the other vehicle was out of sight – to discover her tyres were fully inflated.' This incident echoes similar urban myths around the world, and until some evidence comes to light to prove such a road encounter took place, the story will no doubt remain as folklore.

✳ ✳ ✳

Another of Kent's strangest road-related tales involves the village of Hunton in Maidstone. Now, the following story may sound like a classic urban legend and complete fiction but, according to witness Peter Russell, this was very much a real event. On 20 September 1985, at approximately 11.30 p.m., Mr Russell, a lorry driver, was travelling up Hunton Hill when he ran over the body of a woman who was lying in the road. A doctor and a police officer were already at the scene tending to the body when this terrible incident took place. Peter was traumatised and went to investigate but, bizarrely, was told by the police officer and doctor that he had not killed the girl and that he should simply go home and rest whilst they dealt with the matter. Maybe due to shock, Peter agreed – but so unsettled was he that he decided to ring the local police station. He was told by the officer on duty that there had been no such incident – no police officer or doctor at Hunton Hill, and no report of Mr Russell's unfortunate collision. The officer at the station suggested that maybe Mr Russell had been the victim of a hoax.

This is an incredibly weird story, which reminds me of the case recalled by Iris (*see* p. 51). Even so, this would seem a rather complex hoax without a purpose. In the legend told by Iris, when the motorist got out of the car to look at the 'body', someone then slinked into the unattended vehicle. But why, at such a late hour, would people dressed as a police officer and a doctor wait in the road for someone to hit what I assume was a dummy? This would be a dangerous hoax that could have resulted in death or a bad accident.

In the 1970s, Richard Studholme, guitarist for the band Chicory Tip, claimed he was the victim of a cruel phantom hitch-hiker hoax. He'd been travelling near the Lower Bell region of Blue Bell Hill when he stopped to offer a lift to a young woman, who asked to be taken to West Kingsdown. However, en route the woman asked Richard if he could go to an address in Swanley afterwards to tell her parents she was safe. When Richard dropped the girl off at West Kingsdown he promised he would go to her parents' house, but upon arrival – at quite a late hour – he was told by the man who answered the door that his daughter had died many years ago in a road accident.

If Studholme initially thought that he was the victim of a cruel hoax, then a short while afterwards he began to change his mind, stating: 'It wasn't until some months later that I read in a Kent newspaper of other strange happenings at the spot, that I began to believe I had driven a ghost in my car. I touched the girl. I took her bag from her and helped her into the car ...'

There is a slightly different version of events, maybe due to press confusion, which states that the girl asked Mr Studholme to take her to Bridge Wood – which ties in with the Emily Trigg murder. But, as with so many of these incidents, I guess we'll never get to the truth of the matter.

* * *

During the 1980s, a group of four women travelling up Blue Bell Hill all claimed to have driven straight through a whitish figure that appeared in the road. Can four witnesses all hallucinate the same thing, or were they part of some bizarre supernatural script which plays out every now and then on that old hill? No one is quite sure, but you can guarantee that every 19 November someone will visit the hill hoping to become part of the legend. However, before you start thinking that it's okay to turn off the light, I'll leave you with a strange encounter that took place during the early hours of 11 June 2012, at 12.15 a.m.

A man and his friend were travelling through Blue Bell Hill village during a torrential downpour when suddenly a woman – in her twenties, wearing white and with light-brown shoulder-length hair – ran into the road waving her arms frantically. The man stopped his car and the woman put her hands on the bonnet and began pleading for help.

The woman, clearly in some distress, appeared confused and asked where she was. The driver told her she was at Blue Bell Hill and she replied, 'Where the hell is that?' She then stated that she needed to go to what the witnesses heard as 'Sultan Road', but they had never heard of such a place. The men were rather unnerved by the woman and claimed that she had black eyes, as if mascara had been smudged. The woman then attempted to get into the back of the vehicle – the doors were locked – which also terrified the witnesses, and they persisted in asking her where Sultan Road was. She eventually replied that it was in Snodland (there is no Sultan Road in Snodland, the closest is in Chatham; but there is a Saltings Road in Snodland). The men were rather spooked by the woman and decided to drive away, parking up near to the picnic area at Common Road to calm their nerves. The passenger, who lives in the village, did not want his friend to drive him home in case the woman followed. A short while later, they drove back through the village and saw the woman standing on the disused slip road which leads onto the A229.

The passenger was so scared that he phoned his mother and she told him that maybe the woman had had a row with her partner and been left on the hill, but this seems rather unlikely. A woman in distress in such a spot and at such a late hour during bad weather would surely have knocked on a few doors rather than waiting for a car to pass. It's worth noting that although this may have simply been a 'real' woman left on her own, she was seen in the same area where Chris Dawkins had his encounter. In addition, the slip road situated next to the derelict Upper Bell public house is another area known for sightings. It is also worth mentioning that in the autumn of 1981 a woman was hit by a car and killed further down the hill.

Was this a recent sighting of one of Blue Bell Hill's resident spooks, or simply an extraordinary, but real, event that will no doubt add to the legend? It seems very strange that the incident occurred during June rather than the usual wintry months, but it was awful weather that night – pounding rain – and it's during such storms that some researchers believe ghosts are most likely to appear. Maybe these two men were simply victims of a hoax, but again, this seems too complex to have been a practical joke. And why would someone – particularly a lone woman – loiter around Blue Bell Hill in the middle of the night in the hope that a car would come by? As usual, none of it makes sense, and that's the reason why the mystery continues … and to make matters weirder, several taxi drivers have been called to the eerie spot next to the disused pub in order to pick a woman up. On the phone the fare requested to be taken to Bridge Wood, but each time the taxi turned up there was no one around. Coincidence or something spookier?

THE NECESSARY EVILS OF MODERN TECHNOLOGY

The imagination is an eye, a marvellous third eye that floats free.

✦

Danse Macabre, **Stephen King**

IN 2004 A Japanese movie named *One Missed Call* was released. Directed by Takashi Miike, the film concerns a group of friends who are having a get together one night when one of their mobile phones begins to ring. The owner of the phone, Okasaki Yoko, doesn't recognise the caller and so lets the call go to voicemail. However, when Okasaki looks at the number she notices that, rather oddly, the number displayed is her own … but from two days in the future. Okasaki and her friend listen to the call, and Okasaki recognises her own voice chatting away and then her own horrendous scream. Of course, Okasaki and her friends laugh off the message, believing it to be a hoax – until two days later when Okasaki phones her friend Yumi, who suddenly realises what is about to happen; sure enough, after a short chat Okasaki screams down the phone. Okasaki is thrown under a train by some supernatural force, but her severed hand, still holding the phone, begins to dial a number – that of a friend named Kawai – and this triggers a similar event, and so on and so on.

This eerie chain of events is very much representative of how urban legends are triggered and flow. Clearly mobile phones, along with computers, have become part of the urban legend ring. When mobile phones and PCs became popular, emails were forwarded by mysterious companies, who encouraged users to enter personal details as a way of improving their service. Of course, many of these 'improvements' were nothing more than scams, which many people fell for and still do today. Nowadays it seems as if everyone owns a mobile phone – the latest gadgets seem to almost be an extension of the human body. However, mobile phones are not without their scare stories. In 2005, *BBC News* reported on the 'Petrol station mobile risk myth', as many people believed that turning a mobile phone on in a petrol station forecourt would cause an explosion. Dr Adam Burgess from the University of Kent exposed the urban legend and presented his findings in a conference in March 2005. Burgess' findings showed that, of the 243 petrol station fires caused in eleven years, not one could be attributed to a mobile phone. Strangely, a majority of forecourt fires were, according to a BP fire safety officer, caused by static from the human body.

Adam Burgess told the BBC: 'The petrol station/mobile phone story crosses into the realm of rumour and urban legend. Even on an oil rig, the only real reason not to use a mobile is because of the issue of distraction.'

It would seem that the concept of an ignited cigarette causing a petrol station explosion is also unfounded, as Dr Burgess added that a lit cigarette was not hot enough to ignite petrol. A few years ago rumours were also rife that a mobile phone could be used to fry an egg – although a majority of the public (especially those keen to create scare stories) were more concerned that overuse of phones could in fact fry the brain! Several schools in Kent came forward to express their concerns that mobile phones being used by children could result in diseases such as cancer. Interestingly, the 2000 film *Urban legends: Final Cut* gives coverage to this myth. These legends are commonplace in society and remind us of the days when microwave ovens were considered household hazards. In the 1980s, a Maidstone lady named Miss Hapgood mentioned that a friend of a friend (as always) of hers had attempted to dry off her pet cat by putting it in the microwave. According to Miss Hapgood, the pet owner, not realising the dangers of the microwave, frazzled her animal.

This is of course false – but it is a popular urban legend once again connected to the dangers of modern technology. For every positive thing said about a microwave oven, or mobile phone, there is always a negative, and many scare stories are simply put forward due to people not understanding a new invention that has taken off. In the case of what has become known as The Microwaved Pet, there are numerous stories worldwide concerning people who have allegedly put their small pets into the microwave to dry them off. The variation, of course, is that in some of the legends a child is responsible for putting the pet in, and in some versions it is a baby being mircowaved! Around the time when self-tanning beds became popular, there were fears that people would end up cooking themselves.

Those dreaded microwave tales remind me of a terrifying movie from 1975 called *Trilogy of Terror*, a film which to this day my mum cannot sit through. The film features three short stories; one is called 'Amelia' and concerns a woman (played by Karen Black) who, by accident, knocks a bracelet off a Zuni fetish doll in her apartment, releasing some power within the doll – which suddenly takes on a life of its own. In the movie, we are treated to a climax where Black, after an entire evening of being hounded, slashed and stabbed by the evil troll, shuts the demon in the oven. I distinctly recall my mother shouting at the television screen, 'Don't open the bloody oven!' But, of course, the woman does, and is eventually possessed by the doll. The moral of the story is:

don't open the oven when you've got an evil doll in there. Or, beware the horrors of modern technology!

∗ ∗ ∗

Technology also features in one of the most classic urban legends of all time. I recall being at junior school on a bright summer's day, chatting away to a friend of mine, when a girl rushed over to say that a friend of her aunt had a scary experience over the weekend. Her tale was as follows:

My aunt's friend was babysitting for someone in Strood on Saturday. The two children were upstairs asleep and my aunt's friend was watching television. It was about midnight when the phone rang. My aunt's friend picked the phone up and a man on the other end began breathing heavily and then hung up. My aunt's friend thought it was someone mucking about and it happened again, but the third time the phone rang a man said, 'Are the children okay?' and then laughed and put the phone down. This scared my aunt's friend a bit and so she went upstairs to check the children and found them sound asleep. She came back downstairs, made herself a cup of tea and the phone rang again. The same thing happened, and this time my aunt's friend swore down the phone and hung up. The trouble is, this happened quite a lot, and so eventually my aunt's friend called the operator, told the man about the strange calls and the operator said they would try and trace the call. About five minutes later the operator rang back and said that the call was coming from inside the house!

Now, this is a rather spooky story but it's also classic urban legend material. In America, this urban legend is known

as The Babysitter and the Man Upstairs, but in England
it was made popular by an atmospheric 1979 film called
When A Stranger Calls. This legend has several variations and
is simply fiction – friend-of-a-friend lore never traced back
to one singular origin. When I was told this story, I knew
straightaway it was a myth because I'd already seen the
opening scenes of the creepy thriller involving a woman
being pestered by sinister phone calls, with the operator
eventually confirming that the calls are being made from
inside the house. In other versions, the tormented babysitter
runs upstairs and finds the children slaughtered; in another
version she goes to check on the children but is met by a
man, wielding a bloody knife, coming down the stairs. These
stories are always altered slightly to fit in with the storyteller's
own life, so, in the case I heard, this incident was said to have
taken place in Strood. We never got to find out who the
woman was or what happened after the operator traced the
call, and that's because we were too wrapped up in the twist
that the call was coming from inside the house. Back in the
1970s and '80s, many films and television dramas were based
on similar tales, and these infiltrated our nightmares. The
late 1990s and beyond provided us with modern updates on
such legends, enabling the chain of horror to continue. The
fact that we are able to revolve such horrors around modern
technology means that these stories will always be relevant,
despite the fact the legends themselves are decades old.

⁂ ⁂ ⁂

Back in the late 1970s or early '80s (I don't recall the exact
year, but the vagueness only adds to the legend!) I remember
visiting Chatham High Street with my mum and dad.

THE NECESSARY EVILS OF MODERN TECHNOLOGY

We would often go there to do a spot of shopping and, if I was well behaved, I'd sometimes come home with a new *Star Wars* figure. One afternoon we visited what was known as Alders, a big department store in the High Street. We entered the main door and went on the escalator to the next floor. I used to hate escalators due to the urban legends attached to them. Through friends and family, I heard many horror stories concerning children who'd had limbs and digits torn off after getting items of clothing such as scarves, jumper sleeves and shoe laces caught in the teeth of the ascending or descending steps. These were the sort of scare stories played out on Public Information Films, which used to terrify me as a child. One such film showed a hooded figure – like a monk, but with no visible face – standing near a lake. Actor Donald Pleasence spookily narrated the clip, as a foolish child attempted to retrieve his football from the murky depths. The monk acted as a portent of misfortune, and Pleasence's narration was a warning voice, urging children not to play near dangerous places. Whether it was flying kites too near to pylons, or not respecting escalators in department stores, these were examples of modern technology becoming the bogeyman of urban legend. So imagine my horror when, standing alongside my mum on that escalator, I suddenly lost my footing and fell. Thankfully I wasn't chewed up by the mechanical monster as, despite the legends, this sort of thing rarely happened. But I recall that incident to this day – not just because I expected to look up and see that hideous monk laughing at me for not heeding his warning, but because my mum and dad argued about whose fault it was for the next twenty years!

Elevators, revolving doors, farm and factory machinery, and railway lines all have similar legends attached to them. Just like the mobile phone, these are necessary evils which can, if you believe the stories, become your worst nightmare. Hard to believe that just a few decades ago a whole neighbourhood could be set into panic if a few chain letters were received. Nowadays the inboxes on our essential PCs are frequently plagued by similar threats, warnings and scams, and we rarely bat an eyelid; but years ago, to destroy a chain letter was considered bad luck. For me, the most absurd aspect of the chain-letter phenomenon was the fact that some idiot spent so much time writing and photocopying the letters, and then spent a few quid posting them. Nowadays, a click of a button can send a similar letter to thousands of people.

Another thing that always gets a mention when it comes to technology-related urban myths is plug sockets. Back in the 1950s, '60s and '70s, and to a lesser extent the 1980s, every time there was a severe storm which produced streaks of lightning, people would run around their house making sure all the electrical plugs had been removed from their sockets! In some instances, people would also make sure every door or window of the house was left open, so that lightning could escape should it shoot down from the heavens and aim itself at a certain house. Yes, people and objects have been struck by lightning, but such panic as a way of coping with a force of nature seems absurd. The lightning scares of yesteryear seem almost as dramatic as the panic caused as the year 2000 loomed, and everyone prepared for our computer systems and goodness knows what else to fail.

✳ ✳ ✳

One PC-related urban legend, which brings to mind the classic Babysitter myth, began life as an email chain letter a few years ago. I recall seeing a similar email at a place in

Gillingham where I worked many years ago. Imagine that you are sitting at your work desk and the following email comes through to your inbox:

Subject: Fw: Clown

This creepy or what?

A few years ago a mother and father decided they needed a break so they wanted to head out for a night on the town. So they called their most trusted babysitter. When the babysitter arrived the children were already asleep in bed so the babysitter got to just sit around …

Later in the night the babysitter got bored and decided to see what was on television but she couldn't watch it downstairs as the family didn't have Sky so, to be polite, the babysitter called the parents and asked them if she could watch television in their room, which they were more than happy for her to do. However, before putting the phone down, the babysitter asked the parents if it would be okay to cover up the life-size clown model in the bedroom as it was spooking her … the phone went silent for a few seconds before the couple began telling the babysitter to go and wake the children up and leave the house. The babysitter was unsure why, but the father was eager to get his message across and told the babysitter he would call the police. The babysitter asked why, to which the father responded frantically, 'We don't have a damn clown model …,' but it was too late, the babysitter and the children were murdered.

The email ends with a warning:

If you don't send this email on to five other people in ten minutes then tonight the clown will visit you whilst you're in bed.

Okay, so this legend is a complete rip-off of the babysitter yarn, and it's a rather poor imitation, but it's interesting to note how such an urban legend, over the years, has passed from being an oral tale to a technological chain letter. Mobile phones are also suffering from similar messages; these appear to be more effective, as customers are being asked to perform certain tasks on their phone for added bonuses etc. – but what they do eventually get is a disabled phone. And we can never forget the warning from our parents about what happens when we watch too much TV: our eyes go square. The warnings have always been there with technology. Take heed or die!

✳ ✳ ✳

And lastly, I bring to your attention the tale of the possessed radio. In the June 2012 issue of *Fortean Times* magazine, a man named Chris Kilner wrote in with a peculiar tale. Although Chris now resides in Kenya, in the 1970s he lived in Chatham, and was employed as a milkman. Chris would often cycle to work at around 3 a.m. He stated, 'I would cycle out through the countryside to Gillingham. I used to listen to the birds sing, watch the dawn creeping slowly in and hear the trees swaying as if they were talking to each other.'

One day Chris purchased a second-hand radio from a local market. 'It was one of those small, old ones with knobs that clicked when you turned it off and on.' The night before work, Chris tuned the radio in to BBC Radio 2, turned it off, and placed it in his satchel for the next morning.

Whilst taking in the countryside, as always, Chris was suddenly startled by the radio turning itself on and blasting out at full volume; weirder still, the bike Chris was riding started to travel in circles, as if it had a life of its own. 'I tried to shout, scream even, but nothing happened and I felt as if I was being choked,' Chris told the magazine.

The sudden shrill noise of the radio had somehow triggered a series of surreal events which Chris was now locked into. He added, 'My cycle started to go back the way I had come.'

Chris wrenched his bag from the back of his bike and tossed it into the undergrowth, and then attempted to make his way to work, where a colleague remarked to him that it looked as if he'd seen a ghost. Quite a while later, Chris became a baker for a Gillingham company. Two weeks into his day shift, Chris was told by the manager that he would need to fill in on the night shift – a position that meant Chris would be working on his own. When he had just started work, at 10 p.m., the radio turned on by itself and began 'spouting what sounded like gibberish'. Naturally, this freaked Chris out, especially as it brought to mind the previous experience. But when the pots and pans began to rattle too, Chris became really unsettled. An icy-cold atmosphere filled the room and Chris fled – and didn't return until the next day, when he expected to receive the wrath of the manager. He was pleasantly surprised to find that the reason there had been a vacant slot on the night shift was because the previous baker had left after experiencing strange things!

Maybe it was the bakery that was haunted, but it seems rather odd that both cases involved a radio seemingly having supernatural powers.

DEVILISH LEGENDS 4

Fear of the dark is the most childlike fear ...

✦

Danse Macabre, Stephen King

THE DEVIL HAS embedded his trident into our folklore for centuries, and he is mentioned in several Kent-related urban legends. The first of these comes from Blue Bell Hill.

Blue Bell Hill harbours several mysterious stones which are Neolithic remains. The most notable of these is Kit's Coty House, believed to be the remains of a chambered long barrow, which juts out of the countryside like two gargantuan goalposts bridged by a mighty capstone. Although several legends are attached to these stones, it is the stones at the foot of the hill which harbour the most fascinating urban legend.

These mysterious stones, known as Little Kit's Coty House (or Lower Kit's Coty House), sit in a field close to the village of Aylesford. They are considered to be part of the Medway megaliths and appear as eerie, scattered sarsen boulders that over the years have been bestowed the mystical name of the Countless Stones. The urban legend is that no one, however hard they try, can count the stones. If they ever managed to do so, against all the odds, they would have a meeting with the Devil! A great story indeed, and one that adds to the magic and mystery of this already peculiar place. The English Heritage sign in close proximity states that there are '20 sarsen boulders' and yet, ask anyone – especially children – to count these stones and they seem to come up with a different number every time, usually between eighteen and twenty-three. This is because the way the stones are positioned makes it very difficult to count them.

No one seems to know how on earth these stones ended up scattered around; and it seems strange that Kit's Coty House, a few hundred metres away, is upstanding and yet the Countless Stones are somehow in disarray.

Theories abound as to how and why such stones are situated in the village. Charles Igglesden, in his third volume of *A Saunter through Kent with Pen and Pencil* (1901), wrote of the legend:

> It is said that nobody can count them ... and I must confess that upon visiting the place with three friends the other day, each of us counted the stones and brought out a different total – anything between seventeen and twenty-one. Many, many years ago a certain baker of Aylesford determined to arrive at a correct solution, so he appeared on the scene with a basket full of tiny loaves. Round the pile he went carefully placing a loaf on each stone. So far so good. Next he proceeded to count the loaves and place them in his basket. One, two, three, he picked up and so on, until he reached the last. In a voice of triumph he stooped forward and was about to call aloud the fatal number when with a gasp he fell dead! There is a variation in the story by which the baker, upon counting the stones afterwards, found one more loaf than he brought with him – a weird freak ascribed to the Evil One.

The most contradictory detail about the Countless Stones urban legend is that, if the stones really are *impossible* to count, how on earth could the Devil turn up when you count them correctly? The legend perhaps exists as a warning, to deter people from trespassing in the area or tampering with such mystical arrangements. Various other ancient stones dotted around Britain are said to have the same legend attached.

Kit's Coty House has several weird legends, one suggesting that the stones represent a hidden burial chamber. Another theory is that, on certain nights, fairies and other imps of the darkness emerge from a magic portal within the stones. Others claim that the stones were put there on a stormy night by three witches.

* * *

Kent has another Devil legend attached to its eerie history. The village of Pluckley, mentioned in the Domesday Book of the eleventh century, is said to be one of the most haunted villages in Britain. In a wooded area, or so the urban legend goes, there is a bush known as the Devil's Bush. It is said that if anyone is brave enough to visit the village on a certain night of the year (probably a stormy one around Halloween), and then strip off completely naked and dance backwards around the bush three times, then the Devil will appear. This story has been woven into Pluckley's lore and, like many urban legends, there are several variations. One variation is the number of times the foolish person is said to dance around the bush, and another is whether or not they do so backwards. I'm unsure if anyone has ever been daft enough to test the legend, but, let's face it, if you did visit Pluckley on a cold, blustery and pitch black night, and if you did strip off, perform the ritualistic dance and conjure the dark lord himself, I'm sure the last thing he'd want to see is you standing there, stark naked, staring back at him! The legend is made all the more vague in that no one actually knows where the Devil's Bush is. The village of Pluckley is extremely rural, which would make finding the bush about as easy as looking for a needle in a haystack.

* * *

The historic town of Royal Tunbridge Wells also has a Devil legend. The regal setting is known for curative waters, accessed via a spring situated at a walkway of shops called the Pantiles. The chalybeate spring – discovered in 1606 by Dudley North – offers rich waters, said to have healing powers and iron-like qualities. According to the legend, those who drink the waters will be cured of most ailments, including hangovers, obesity and 'a moist brain'. The Devil has strong connections with the spring because it was said that many years ago, when the Horned One was visiting Sussex, he had a run-in with St Dunstan, who clamped a set of hot blacksmith tongs over the nostrils of the Devil and sent him packing. To relieve himself of his scorched nose, Satan loped away to Tunbridge Wells and dipped his burning nostrils into the spring. And from then on the waters were said to have a reddish hue. The following verse was penned about the waters:

These waters youth in age renew
Strength to the weak and sickly add
Give the pale cheek a rosy hue
And cheerful spirits to the sad.

There are several spots in Kent said to harbour healing waters, all of which have legends attached to them. One particular spring is said to be located at Pizien Well Road in the village of Wateringbury. The name of Pizien may well derive from 'poison', but the waters are far from hostile. Legend has it that, many years ago, newly wedded couples would visit the waters and sip from them in order to ensure fertility. Other magical waters have been mentioned at Harbledown, a village that is the last resting place for pilgrims en route to Canterbury. At one spot is the Black Prince's Well, so-called because the prince would take a flask from there every day. At Otford sits another miraculous well, Becket's Well. The legend states that when Archbishop Thomas á Becket visited the area, he was most upset at the lack of quality water and so struck the ground with his crozier. From then on, two springs bubbled from that spot. At Dungeness, on the Kent coast, there is a strange legend which states that during severe storms witches fly through the air on broomsticks; some of their comrades were said to have once flown over the village of Rolvenden, particularly in the region of St Mary the Virgin Church, in order to steal the holy water. Another watery legend comes from the village of Wye, where a holy well near Brook Road is said to contain blessed waters. Charles Igglesden has written of the remedial spring, stating: 'It is recorded that a dropsical woman who drank of the waters vomited two black toads, which changed into dogs and then asses ...' Poor woman!

The Devil also has connections to an urban legend from the Maidstone village of Loose. Situated in this tranquil and picturesque setting is All Saints' Church. In the churchyard is a pillar memorial to the Charlton family of Pimps Court and atop it can be seen three horrible faces, which many years ago were etched into the stone as a way of warding off the Devil. It is claimed that if you visit the churchyard at midnight, stick a pin in the old yew tree there, run around it anti-clockwise twelve times, and then quickly gaze into the smaller window situated above the Charlton memorial, then you will see a face. Some say the face is that of the Devil, whilst others claim it is the missing fourth face from the pillar. An older, more gruesome, telling of the legend claims that after sticking the pin into the tree and running round it twenty-four times, if you peer through the trefoil window you will see the horrifying sight of a woman murdering a baby. To some extent this legend reminds us of Bloody Mary, but instead of staring into a mirror in the dark, one looks through a window. Most of these legends involve running around something, or doing a ritual at a certain time, and always on a dark, eerie night.

At Nettlestead, also in Maidstone, it is said that if you observe a certain footpath that leads to the river, on a specific night of the year – usually around 11 November – then you will see the materialisation of a trio of ghosts, the first being a phantom bridge, the second being a ghostly monk which appears on the bridge (*see* Chapter Seven for more monk-related legends), and the third being a spectral woman – bound and gagged – who is then tossed into the inky waters of the river by the monk. Seconds later the image fades.

Like many other urban legends, these tales seem to exist as dares, or as cautionary tales not to visit certain areas. Historian Jackie Grebby mentions another Devil legend on her 'Exploring Kent History' blog:

Michaelmas is on 29 September. It means very little to most people nowadays, but it used to herald important events in rural tradition. From the Middle Ages until at least the seventeenth or eighteenth centuries it marked the expected end of the harvest when a goose, fattened on the grain left on the fields after the harvest, was enjoyed. In my family it is the day before Michaelmas that has some importance. It was my grandmother's birthday and she always said: 'Never pick blackberries after my birthday as they belong to the Devil.' (The usual countryside belief is that come Michaelmas night, the Devil spits on them.)

The Devil also made his mark – quite literally, or so they say – in Newington. It was here, at St Mary the Virgin Church, that the Devil is said to have left his hoofprint many years ago.

One day, the local priest claimed to his fellow wardens that he had been visited by Satan. The Devil, according to the priest, had visited the church as he was unhappy at the constant ringing of the bells and warned that the clamour must stop immediately. The priest described the Devil as being jet black in colour, from head to toe, with not a strand of hair visible anywhere, and with a beak for a nose and a long tail with a fork on the end. This unholy visitation upset the local community terribly and they all pulled together, wondering how on earth they could keep the miserable creature from returning. As they were unwilling to put a halt to the ringing of the church bells, the bells continued to ring across the village for many months. The weird incident was forgotten until a very stormy summer came round and brought with it another visitation from Satan – and such a severe thunderstorm that all the local crops were destroyed. Villagers ran to pray as the rains came down, and although the storm ceased, shortly afterwards a terrible drought hit Newington, whilst neighbouring villages and their crops flourished. It seemed that the Devil was extremely unhappy that the wardens had not ceased the ringing of the church bells, and he sought to punish the whole community.

One night the priest observed the Devil standing in the porch of the church. Satan had his hands over his ears, trying to prevent the holy ringing from entering his pounding head. The Devil then left the church but returned a few nights later, this time armed with a sack, in which he attempted to put the church bells. According to the legend, Satan lost his balance due to the weight of the bells and fell to the ground; he released his grip on the sack, which opened and spilled the bells into the stream – hence the fact that the stream is now said to bubble and the bells ring purely. As a mark of this event, there is said to be a strange impression in the stone close to the gate; it measures 15in in length and many believe it to be the footprint of the Devil himself. One legend states that the stone sparkles if struck.

A different version of events is that the the wardens decided one night to sell the great bell to pay for the damage done to the other bells. The wardens knew that selling the bell would upset the locals, so they decided to remove it at night. They raised the bell to the roof of the tower in order to lower it down the outside – but whilst in the act, the Devil suddenly appeared and grabbed hold of the bell. However, the Devil soon fled, and although the men tried on several occasions to raise the bell, they repeatedly failed. They sought advice from a local witch, who told the wardens that the only way to raise the great bell would be to have it drawn by four great white oxen. The wardens almost succeeded in their quest until a local urchin walked by and shouted, 'Look at the black spot behind that bull's ear,' and with that the wardens lost concentration, dropped the bell, and it was never seen again.

A few miles away from Newington is Rainham. The church here is said to have once been attacked by the Devil, who tried to push the tower over. Legend has it that several visible marks on the tower and churchyard wall were made by Satan. Or has this legend become confused with that of Newington?

It is also claimed that the town of Whitstable exists because of Satan. An anonymous writer, contributing to the *Gentleman's Magazine*, stated:

While strolling on the Kentish coast last summer I halted at a roadside inn, in what I found was styled West end of Herne I inquired, among other matters, the distance to Whitstable, and received the desired information from the portly, good natured-looking mistress with the addition, 'Ah, sir, that's a queer place you'll see all the houses stuck up and down the hill, just as the devil dropped 'em, as folk say here.' I naturally asked the particulars of this diabolical feat, and in answer was favoured with the following tale, which I do not give in the good lady's own words, lest I should wound the *amour propre* of the respected citizens of Durovernum, for, according to her, 'it was all along of the wickedness of the Canterbury people,' of which some instances were supplied.

Canterbury, as all the world of Kent knows, is 'no mean city' now, but six centuries ago, when it was the resort of thousands of pilgrims, it was so glorious that it excited the wrath of the foul fiend, and its inhabitants being as bad as Jerome describes the people of Jerusalem to have been when that city too was famous for pilgrimages he sought and obtained permission to cast it into the sea, if the service of prayer and praise usually performed by night and by day at the tomb of St. Thomas the Martyr should he once suspended. Long and eagerly did Satan watch, but though the people grew worse and worse daily, the religious were faithful to their duties, and he almost gave up the hope of submerging the proud city. At length, however, his time came. A great festival had been held at which the chaplains at the saint's tomb had of course borne a prominent part, and when night came, utterly exhausted, they slept – all, and every one.

The glory of Canterbury was now gone for ever. Down pounced the fiend and endeavoured to grasp the city in his arms, but though provided with claws proverbially long, he was unable to embrace one half, so vast was its size. A portion, however, he seized, and having with a few strokes of his wings reached the open sea, he cast in his evil burden. Thrice he repeated his journey, portion after portion was sunk, and the city was all but annihilated, when the prayers of the neglected St. Thomas prevailed, and an angelic vision was sent to Brother Hubert the Sacristan, which roused and directed him what to do. He rushed into the church, and seizing the bell-rope, he pulled vigorously. The great bell, Harry, which gives its name to the centre tower of the minster, ordinarily required the exertions of ten men to set it in motion, but it now yielded to the touch of one, and a loud boom from its consecrated metal scared the fiend just as he reached the verge of the sea. In despair he dropped his prey and fled, and Canterbury has never since excited his envy by its splendour.

There was a remarkable difference in the fate of the different parts of Satan's last armful, from which a great moral lesson was justly drawn by my informant. Those very few houses in which more good than bad were found were preserved from destruction by falling on the hill-side, and they thus gave rise to the thriving port of Whitstable while the majority, where the proportions were reversed, dropped into the sea a mile off, and there their remains are still to be seen, but antiquaries, if ignorant of the facts of the case, have mistaken them for the ruins of Roman edifices submerged by the encroaching ocean.

∗ ∗ ∗

Another Devil legend is attached to an ancient structure known as High Rocks, situated in Tunbridge Wells. Today it is used by rock climbers, but in the past a young woman once fell under the spell of the Devil here. Satan had disguised himself as a handsome young fellow and, to stop the young woman leaving, he ensnared her hand in the tentacles of an old oak tree then attempted to grope her. However, the woman had an advantage over Lucifer, for in her hand she held three drops of crystal-clear water which entitled her to one wish. Sadly, before making a wish to free herself, the woman caught the gaze of the young man, became bewitched by him and was turned to stone. An engraving on the nearby Wishing Stone reads:

Pause ere you wish
From idle wish refrain,
For what you wished,
Not wish you wished, you gain

Although the tale of the Devil's Oak appears old, it has spawned a modern urban legend. This states that couples who visit the spot can test their love, by clasping hands and passing them through the gnarled roots of the tree. If their hands emerge from the roots still clasped then their love will last eternal. Another legend dares the adventurer to collect three droplets of water and make a wish, but warns that the last person to do this was molested by Satan and turned into stone.

Elsewhere in Tunbridge Wells one can find Wellington Rocks, another huge sandstone rock formation. A romantic legend is attached to these grey stones, for it is said that almost a century ago, in 1917, two young lovers named Daniel and Elaine frequented this spot. One day Daniel received his call-up papers for war, but promised his love that he would return some day to marry her. A while passed but one day Elaine was contacted by Daniel's mother, who told her that Daniel would be coming home, and so Elaine rushed to the rocks and waited for him. Sadly, Daniel never turned up; he had been killed at war and Elaine, alone with her sorrow in the pouring rain and blustery gales, fell from the rocks and died. Legend claims that if you visit Wellington Rocks on certain nights of the year, when the clouds are grey, the rain falls hard and the wind howls, you can hear Elaine's voice, yearning for her long-lost love.

The Chiding Stone at Chiddingstone is another peculiar block of sandstone with a mystical aura. No one really knows why the rock is the shape it is or how it got there, and so, as in many cases, people have put forward their own theories, in turn creating legends about the spot. Like the stones of Little Kit's Coty, some believe that the Chiding Stone was once used as an altar, possibly by the Druids; a less dramatic theory states it is simply a boundary marker dating back to Saxon times.

It would seem that another reason, especially in Kent, that we have so many not just ghost stories, but urban legends, is because of the smuggling trade. Centuries ago smugglers operated around the coastal areas of Kent, particularly in spots such as Romney Marsh and Ashford, when parts were close to the water. It is said that many creepy legends were created by local smugglers in order to keep people away from remote areas which hid their illegal goods.

In M.R. James' brilliantly eerie ghost story *A Warning to the Curious*, we meet an amateur archaeologist who visits a windswept coastline in order to search for an ancient lost crown. Eventually, after a nightly dig, he discovers the artefact – but also disturbs a nefarious entity which subsequently stalks him. This legend brings to mind a similar tale from the village of Aldington in Ashford, where it is said that many years ago an urban legend was created as a way of warning people away from the place where a valuable crown was hidden. One reckless trespasser sought the treasure in an area known as The Knoll, described as follows by the poet Hueffer:

> Al'ington Knoll it stands up high,
> Guidin' the sailors sailin' by,
> Stands up high fer all to see,
> Cater the marsh and crost the sea.
> Al'ington Knoll's a mound a top,
> With a dick all round and it's bound to stop,
> For them as made it in them old days,
> Sees to it well that theer it stays.
> For that ol' Knoll is watched so well,
> By drowned men let outen Hell,
> They watches well and keeps it whole,
> For a sailor's mark – the goodly Knoll.
> Farmer Finn as farms the ground,
> Tried to level that goodly mound,
> But not a chap from Lydd to Lym'
> Thought that job were meant for him.
> Finn 'e fetched a chap fro' th' Sheeres,
> One o'yer spunky devil-may-kneeres,
> Giv' him a shovel and pick and spade,
> Promised him double what we was paid.
> He digged till ten, and he muddled on,
> Till he'd digged up a sword and a skillington –

A grit old sword as long as me,

An' grit ol' bones as you could see.

He digged and digged the livelong day,

Till the sun went down in Fairlight Bay;

He digged and digged, and behind his back,

The lamps shone out and the marsh went black.

And the sky in the west went black to red,

And the wood went black – and the man was dead,

But where he'd digged the chalk shone white,

Out to see like Calais hight.

Al'ington Knoll it stands up high,

Guidin' the sailors sailin' by,

Stands up high for all to see,

Cater the marsh and crost the sea.

So, urban legends have been with us for centuries, and they cross over into ghostly tales, superstition, folklore and belief. They exist to test our bravery and try to warn us from danger or misdeeds. Take for instance the urban legend connected to Angley Park at Cranbrook, which states that any man who betrays his lover, and visits the area shortly afterwards, will be feasted upon by a tremendous dragon! Of course, dragons have never existed – or have they? Chronicler Charles Igglesden wrote: 'on certain or uncertain nights of the year it wings its flight over the park and pays a visit to the big lake yonder.' Again, there is the element of vagueness, for we are not interested in exact dates (although some say the legend stems from the nineteenth century as the lake was constructed around 1812), and confronts us with the unknown.

For many years there has been an equally bizarre urban legend concerning the unusual grotesques which sit atop the church tower of the Holy Cross Church at Bearsted in Maidstone. No one seems to know what creatures they are – some assume bears, others dogs – but all we are really interested in is the alleged fact that on certain nights of the year, when the church clock strikes midnight, these stone beasts leap down from their perch and wander around the grounds searching for food. A great legend, but if anyone cares to examine it more closely they will find that there is no clock on the church!

Another ghoulish legend concerns a mysterious figure known as the Leaf Man – a creation designed to keep adventurous children away from dangerous places. The village of Aylesham has harboured this legend since the Second World War, when bombs fell on the area. Due to the hazards created by the numerous bomb-holes, parents and grandparents created this bogeyman to keep their brazen kin away from the area of Spinney Wood. And so the legend of the Leaf Man was born, a terrifying apparition said to stand guard over the bomb-holes. Of course, according to some, the Leaf Man was simply a camouflaged soldier. However, if you go down to the woods today you're sure of a big surprise, so my advice is to stay away from Spinney Wood. Also, beware the Bogman. This weirdly named critter was an urban legend created in the Upchurch area of Kent around the 1930s. The Bogman was said to be the spirit of a Neolithic hunter whose mummified remains were found on the marshes, and may have been housed at various locations throughout Medway. During the 1930s it was rumoured that a young girl went missing and, when the corpse of the Bogman was dug up during a police search, in the crumpled hand of the skeleton was a child's shoe. Many years later, when the body of the missing youth was found, she was missing a shoe – a red sandal, exactly the same as the shoe found in the hand of the skeleton. The dreaded Bogman was said to haunt various sites throughout Kent, accompanied by a spectral dog or two. The creature was often described as walking or running with a peculiar gait, caused by the fact that its head flopped backwards, suggesting that in life the figure had been strangled to the point of total decapitation. Interestingly, the Bogman legend bears some similarity to the Leaf Man myth in that it stems from the Second World War, when his remains were allegedly housed at Rochester Museum. The grim exhibit supposedly came to life and escaped, and was said to roam the tunnels of Fort Amherst and Fort Pitt.

In *Medway Towns*, William Hamper claims that the ghost of the Bogman was exorcised in the 1950s, but this didn't stop strange rumours circulating amongst the local schoolgirls of the area. Hamper adds, 'There was even one report of a twelve-year-old girl having her sandal stolen in broad daylight.'

It's difficult to determine how such peculiar, and at times terrifying, legends come about. In June 2012 I was put in touch with a Cuxton resident named Alex Wilson, who told me about a horrifying legend known as Mr Buzz. According to Alex, 'The story goes that there was a rather weird guy, who would walk around the village with a box of flies around his neck.' The man was known to collect flies in the box, and, no doubt due to their buzzing sound, the name Mr Buzz came about. Mind you, just like the Bogman, Mr Buzz was said to be a very evil soul. Alex continued, 'One night a young girl went missing and people searched for her. When her body was found she wasn't alone – Mr Buzz had killed the girl and drilled holes into her spine and was blowing into it which made a horrible buzzing noise.'

I asked Alex where such a macabre legend could have originated from, but she replied, 'I don't know, but it used to give me nightmares.' Another bogeyman – or, more correctly, bogeywoman – legend created to keep children away from dark places is what I knew, as a teenager, as the Reggae Woman. This terrifying apparition, also known as the Voodoo Woman, was said to haunt a stretch of woodland between Rochester and Blue Bell Hill. This urban legend, told to me in the 1990s by a friend at the time named Tom, claimed that certain spots of the woods were frequented by this hideous spectre, who was adorned in an assortment of beads and the like. The beating of her feet could reportedly be heard as she sprinted through the foggy woods. This legend slowly transformed into another legend known as Thumper, said to be a giant, spectral rabbit that would make itself known by beating its hind foot on the ground.

Creepy stuff, and certainly the sort of figure that would keep us away from particular locations. This type of bogeyman reminds me of what became known in America as phantom clowns. A lot of people fear clowns – maybe it's the cracked smile behind the white face, or the fact that films such as *It* have played on this comedy/tragedy figure. Mind you, since the 1980s there have been reports in certain American States of people – especially children – being chased, or even abducted, by such red-nosed lunatics. Of course, in most cases there is nothing to substantiate the alleged incidents. In my hometown of Chatham I distinctly recall a certain ice-cream man who always gave some of the local schoolkids the creeps. Someone had spread a rumour that, in exchange for some bubblegum, a local girl had promised to give the ice-cream man a sexual favour. The poor guy probably hadn't put a foot wrong, but suddenly he found himself part of a vicious smear campaign – which probably didn't do his business much good!

One of the craziest urban legends I've ever encountered came from my old school, Oaklands Infants, which I attended in the early 1980s. I recall one afternoon one of the pupils, a girl named Melissa, saying that she'd gone to the toilet and seen a squirrel, the size of a human, wielding a razor blade! 'Ridiculous!' I hear you cry, and I agree, but many of the kids at the time were absolutely petrified of going to the toilet in case they encountered this surreal monster. The story spread like wildfire, but I guess it petered out when children couldn't put off going to the loo any longer. They probably converged upon the toilets all at once, eager to relieve themselves but also keen to dismiss the legend. However far-fetched the story seems, it echoes familiar toilet terrors from around the country; and schools (*see* Chapter Five) are perfect places for ghost stories and urban legends to start, and very quickly spread. Whether it's the rumour of a spectral caretaker, the legend of a ghostly ex-pupil, or even a myth pertaining to a weird animal or so-called monster prowling outside school gates, the *Scooby-Doo* ingredient seems vital.

As a kid, after flushing the toilet at my parents' house I would run downstairs as if my life depended on it. Did I run because I feared the bogeyman? Did I jump down the steps because I didn't want to look back up the dark stairs? Or did I run because the noise of the flushing toilet, deep down in my mind, sounded like some roaring monster? Maybe, as a friend of mine once theorised, we panic because the sound of the chain flushing obscures any other sound there may be.

For many years, *Fortean Times* has been exploring legends and the paranormal. On the magazine's website is a message board full of stories submitted by readers. One chap, who did not give his name, believed that the sound of the toilet cistern was something akin to an unearthly scream.

Another quirky legend comes from a good friend of mine named Terry Cameron, who told me that when he was at school in Chatham in the 1980s, he was informed that an old black sack in a nearby tree was said to be the exact spot where Dracula was hanged! Terry told me in May 2012, 'This sounds like a silly story but it's one that always stayed with me!'

This vampiric urban legend brings to mind the tale of the 'Gorbals vampire', which I feel I must mention, even though it concerns the city of Glasgow in Scotland; this proves how easily urban legends can spread. The 'Gorbals vampire' scare took place in 1954 after several schoolchildren claimed that an iron-toothed fiend was roaming a local cemetery and had killed and eaten two girls. Youngsters, armed with sticks and stones, swarmed to the site, scaling the 8ft-high walls of the cemetery to search for the 'vampire'. But their hunt proved futile. Government officials blamed the scare on horror comics and movies showing in local theatres.

It seems that we always have to be aware of the bogeyman, and the bogeyman's identity is constantly altering in order to prey on our fear. A decade or so ago, in America, there was mass panic following the rumour that satanists were abducting children for their clandestine midnight manoeuvres. These claims were completely unfounded – in the same way that during the 1980s and '90s, bogus social workers were allegedly being hunted by police for attempted child abduction. Kent got caught up in this brief scare, which tends to surface every few years.

✳ ✳ ✳

Back in 1986 I took an interest in the Devil's music – heavy metal! I distinctly remember a time when heavy metal was very much classed as the soundtrack to Hell created by Beelzebub himself. Heavy metal certainly changed my life, but in a positive way. However, one urban legend which sprouted from the scene, especially in the 1980s, was that all the musicians involved in the genre were satanists and that the records' lyrics possessed teenagers, who in turn would become the Devil's disciples. In the 1980s, heavy metal faced a great deal of opposition, especially in America from groups such as the PMRC, an American censorship committee. But, just like the kid who was warned not to go into the woods but did, I embraced heavy metal music. The problem was, of course, that it was seen as a rebellion and abnormal, and the satanic imagery caused a lot of fuss. Thankfully I was born to two open-minded and loving parents, but I'll never forget the cringeworthy day in McDonald's in Chatham when my cousin, fellow 'metalhead' Jez, turned to his dad and said, 'Dad, there's something I need to tell you – I'm a satanist,' to which his dad replied, 'Well, maybe you should go and see a doctor then.'

In the 1980s, rock stars were getting sued by parents when youngsters committed suicide after listening to heavy metal albums. Of course, the fact that the youths were either out of their head on drugs or drink mattered not to the censors, who blamed the lyrics of heavy metal songs. When I got into heavy metal, the main urban legend – which was a great way of selling records – was that certain albums (we always bought vinyl, not CDs or any of this downloadable malarkey!) contained backwards messages. If any headbanger was brave enough to listen to a record in a candle-lit room (purely for the atmosphere) and play a certain segment of the record backwards, then the Devil was said to appear. Amazingly, many people took this legend seriously, and it was bolstered by the fact that a lot of heavy metal records *did* have strange subliminal messages within their waxy grooves – though these were all nonsense and were included as a gimmick. I recall buying Mötley Crüe's second album, *Shout at the Devil*, because a) the black cover had an upside down pentagram on it – I was a sucker for imagery – and b) the text on the back stated that 'This record may contain backwards messages'. Sadly, it didn't; yet people still bought it in their droves. Thank goodness it was a quality record, or some fans might have felt robbed! Those were the good ol' days – the nights sat in a stuffy, poster-covered room with some cheesy record spinning on the decks. I'll never forget the night I lit some candles (black ones, of course) in my bedroom and stabbed one into a plastic skull I had on a shelf. I started to play a record, in the hope of invoking some rancid demon, when suddenly a burning smell filled the air. At first I thought some evil spectre had emerged from the speakers. Then I checked the plugs and wires of the stereo for a short fuse, and even creaked open my bedroom door to check the smell wasn't coming from the oven downstairs. But then, to my horror, I realised that the candle I'd put into the plastic skull had melted onto it. The skull was now a deformed melting mess, black smoke was billowing from it, and a dark patch had formed on the ceiling. Hardly a ritual I would recommend to aspiring heavy metal fans!

In the 1980s, heavy metal became a cultural bogeyman and, to this day (though to a far lesser extent), it still is. In the 1980s this sound was new, refreshing and downright scary for some, and when something has that type of aura, legends are attached to it.

Much of what I've spoken about has links to childhood, and with that I'd like to move on to more urban legends related to schools. But, before I do, I will finish with another Devil-related urban legend. There is an obscure and rather odd rhyme regarding fingernails, and the cutting thereof, which seems fitting to complete this segment:

Cut them on Monday, cut them for news
Cut them on Tuesday, for new pair of shoes,
Cut them on Wednesday, cut for a letter
Cut them on Thursday, for something better,
Cut them on Friday, cut them for sorrow
Cut them on Saturday, see a loved one tomorrow,
Cut them on Sunday, your safety go seek
For Satan will have you the whole of your week!

SCHOOL LEGENDS

5

... kids are the perfect audience for horror.

✦

Danse Macabre, Stephen King

THE LATE 1970S and early '80s was a time of surreal and scary programmes on television, and horrendous fashion, but a good time was had by all ... unless of course you were affected by urban legends.

One of the most terrifying urban legends during my school years concerned a mythical group of thugs called the Chelsea Smilers. My God, how we feared such imaginary hooligans. I'm not sure where or how it began, but the legend of the Chelsea Smilers seems common to people from all over Britain who experienced the 1980s. It wasn't all Duran Duran and Spandau Ballet! I was a huge football fan and supported Liverpool Football Club from a very early age, but because I watched so much football, I was totally aware of the hooliganism at the time. So can you imagine my, and most of my peers', horror when rumours began to circulate that a vile gang of skinheads were going to be waiting outside the school gates at home time. The rumour spread like wildfire. We knew that football thugs existed but the fact that these yobs were coming to our school brought the reality crashing home. I remember the fuss this legend caused, as some of the kids began running around the classroom in terror, gazing out of the window towards the gates, hoping that at the end of the day their parents would be there to pick them up.

The Chelsea Smilers were said to travel around the country in blue vans (in other versions of the legend these thugs weren't hooligans but violent gypsies), reminding us of the alleged child abductors said to patrol housing estates in white vans, or the creepy clowns of American lore also said to drive around in white vans – or even ice-cream vans! Apparently, these Chelsea Smilers would make the journey down from London, dressed in bovver boots, bleached blue jeans and bomber jackets, sporting a shaved head and displaying hideous scars and tattoos over their bodies. They were a very real bogeyman, not some mythical monster that lived in the woods; the Chelsea Smilers were grotty, evil lunatics, armed with razor blades or Stanley knives, with a reputation for slashing their victims across the mouth, then kneeing them in their private parts – making their victims scream and in turn split their mouths. The other rumour, later on, was that the formidable gang of brutes would use credit cards to slash the mouths of their victims. Ouch!

The Chelsea Smilers never did come to our school but the fear of them was huge. In fact, this was one of the most frightening and seemingly realistic urban legends I've ever experienced, and one that seemed to last for years. I recall the relief on some of the kids' faces as they scurried out of the school gates like frightened mice, desperate to catch a sign of their parents' car. And then there were people like me, who had to walk home. Bizarrely, none of us ever questioned why these thugs wanted to come to our school; after all, why would these villains waste their time, and weapons, on kids when there were probably other gangs they could fight? We never questioned their motives, or where they came from, but we feared them. In some cases across the country the Smilers used to – allegedly – go around headbutting people. This legend no doubt stemmed from terms such as 'Glasgow Kiss', 'Glasgow Smile' and 'Chelsea Grin', which were euphemisms for a headbutt, or for slashing the mouth with a sharp weapon such as a piece of glass or knife.

I've no doubt that the Chelsea Smile was a real act carried out at some point by a mindless gang. Whether true or not, the thought of this gang instilled great fear. As did the rumour that a flasher, or some other sexual deviant, was hanging around outside the school gates. I'm sure – or it may just be legend! – that there were rumours of a man in a white van harassing some of the schoolkids, and it might even have been mentioned in a school newsletter, but no pervert was ever arrested. A similar urban legend, and one that always stuck in my mind whilst attending Walderslade Boys' School in the mid to late 1980s, was the rumour that in the wooded area of the grounds there lurked a man carrying a chain, who, according to one kid, 'Had grabbed one of the girls and dragged her off to the woods …'

In America, the urban legends surrounding schools or college campuses seem far more dramatic and less terrifying than British scares. For instance, at an elementary school in Sayville, New York, a creature known as Noodleman is said to prowl the long, cold corridors. For me, the name of the creature alone is hilarious, rather than scary. The same could be said for the Hoboken Monkey Man, a weird bipedal creature said to have spooked children at a New Jersey school in 1982. These weren't the sort of urban legends to bring nightmares.

On 28 April 2011 the *Sittingbourne Messenger* ran the story: 'Supermarket abduction is a hoax', after an urban legend had circulated on a social networking site that a young child had been grabbed in a supermarket by a 'foreign gang', who had disguised the child in a wig and clothing from the store and bundled them into a van. The article, continued: 'The store is issuing a plea to customers not to be taken in by the story, and the company's head office has also put a message on its website urging parents not to believe the urban myth.'

This wasn't the first time that such a myth had done the rounds. In 2008 a supermarket at Manston was at the centre of a child abduction hoax. The Kent press of 27 June reported: 'Police condemn hoax child abduction story.' Again the power of social networking sites was blamed by officials, who stated that a hoax had begun to circulate that a child had been grabbed in a supermarket car park whilst her mother's back was turned. Superintendent Chris Hogben commented: 'People in East Kent can be assured that if an incident of this nature had taken place, we would be very quick to warn them of it. This irresponsible act has caused angst and distress among parents of young children.'

In most of these cases, no one sees the alleged culprit and vehicle registration numbers are never taken – usually because the assailants do not exist! My sister Vicki, who went to Walderslade Girls' School in the 1990s, told me of a similar threat she heard there. It was rumoured that an old woman (who the pupils called 'Old Nanny') was seen loitering in the woods. According to my sister, it was even speculated that the scary old hag lived somewhere in the woods in a small wooden hut – which is absurd, considering there were hardly any woods to speak of – but again, we come back to the creation of a bogeyman whose purpose is to deter us from visiting the dark corners. We feel safe in school to some extent … but outside the window are woods. As a child in the 1960s, my father, Ron, often visited the Great Lines (a steep hill overlooking Chatham) to find lizards. Many of the local kids were wary of straying close to the property of a man named 'Old Blood', because, as my dad told me, 'If you did go too close he'd get you!'

Looking back I now wonder if such stories were actually created by the schools themselves as a clever ploy to stop children from straying too far at lunchtime! Mind you, I'll add a hint of reality to my sister's legend, because there really was a terrifying local woman when I was growing up, who would spend her time walking the streets and woods of Medway dressed in black, with a white powdered face and a silvery headband. The woman was tall, thin, and looked for all the world like a ghost. I'll never forget the day I was travelling with my dad through a semi-rural area when we saw this strange woman walking along an isolated road dragging a bush! This woman, who some say lost a child many years ago and became tormented by it, was at times a reclusive character, who I imagine might have looked a scary sight if seen walking the eerie lanes around Blue Bell Hill. I don't know what happened to her but some characters are remembered more than others, and a folkloric aura tends to surround them. She brings to mind a verse from Thomas Ingoldsby's poem, 'The Lay of the Old Woman Clothed in Grey':

> Once there lived, as I've heard people say,
> An Old Woman clothed in grey,
> So furrow'd with care,
> So haggard her 'air,
> In her eye such a wild supernatural stare,
> That all who espied her,
> Immediately shied her,
> And strove to get out of her way.

* * *

School was always a hotbed of rumour and speculation. A boy named David at my school asked me if I'd heard about the girl who wore braces on her teeth, who had kissed a guy who also wore braces; they got so badly locked together that an ambulance had to be called. Then there was the horror story (of unspecified date) concerning the boy who, during exam time, had become so stressed by his paper that he put two pencils up his nose (pointed ends first) and slammed his head onto the desk, causing the pencils to pierce his brain.

On 7 March 2012 Kent Online ran the headline: 'Schools in crystal meth sweets hoax', after it was claimed that sweets eaten by local children were being contaminated with the killer drug. The website added: 'Kent police have issued a statement quashing the gossip that has spread through the county as a hoax.'

Due to the power of the playground and social networking sites, such rumours have been causing panic for many years. The deadly sweets doing the rounds were, according to the legend, called Strawberry Quick and Strawberry Meth, but Inspector Ian Sandwell of Kent Police commented that the sweets were 'nothing more than an urban myth'. This scare echoed a similar panic from my schooldays, when it was rumoured that certain sweets being passed around schools were laced with LSD (Lysergic acid diethylamide). Later on this would transform into the slightly different urban legend that business cards put into phone boxes were laced with LSD – or in some cases razor blades!

* * *

Many pupils had the aim of finishing school and going on to college. I opted for Sixth Form, but one fellow I knew, who was a lot older than us boys, told us not to go to college because of something that had happened to a friend of his friend. According to our storyteller, this friend of a friend had gone to college and then on to university far away from home, and was sharing a flat with another guy. One night one of the guys said he was going out on a date and told the other he'd be back late. The guy staying home retired to bed early to read, and fell asleep. During the early hours, the sleeping student was woken up by a scratching and gurgling noise coming from outside the door, but, thinking it was his mate playing a prank, he ignored it and fell back to sleep. When the morning came round he got out of bed, opened the door into the hallway, and, lying there in a pool of blood, was his friend; the gurgling noise had been caused by a deep laceration to the throat and the scratching was his friend attempting to get back in! A shocker of a story, but once again untrue. In fact, this legend can be traced back to America in the 1960s, and has become known as The Room-mate's Death. In some versions the story centres upon two girls, and the one who is sleeping will wake at night and hear a dripping sound. Not wanting to get up and turn the light on, she falls back to sleep; a few hours later she wakes, switches the lamp on, and, to her horror, sees her room-mate bleeding to death on the floor.

The Room-mate's Death probably hasn't happened to anyone, and has echoes of The Boyfriend's Death in the sense that the person who is left behind is tormented by strange scratching noises, which turn out to be their friend dead, or dying.

Most of us schoolkids – even those of us who enjoyed school – couldn't wait to reach the age of eighteen so we could be free agents and go to local pubs and clubs. Mind you, one particular and very sinister rumour which almost put us off going clubbing as we reached our later teenage years was the legend that became known as Welcome to the AIDS Club. The story we heard was that the friend of a friend's sister had been out at a local club (location/date not stated, as always) somewhere near the Medway Towns. Whilst dancing on the crowded floor, the girl felt a pinprick on her hand. She thought nothing of it until she got home and found a note in her pocket saying: Welcome to the AIDS Club. It seems that some unhinged individual had been going round infecting people by pricking them with a syringe. Can you imagine the upset this caused at the time? It did for nightclubs what the movie *Jaws* did for skinny-dipping in the sea! According to Wikipedia: '... the idea that people infected with AIDS have deliberately attempted to infect others in this manner is generally considered an urban legend. There is to date, only one documented case of a pin prick attack leading directly to the transmission of HIV.'

There is another myth known as AIDS Mary which we heard about at school. This was said to concern the friend of a friend's brother, who one night met a gorgeous girl (named Mary) at a local club and took her back to his flat for a one-night stand. He woke to find the woman had gone but had left a message, written in lipstick on the mirror, stating: Welcome to the AIDS Club.

* * *

Another legend going around schools in the 1980s concerned what became known as 'video nasties'. Now, most kids in their mid-teens were exposed to this legend, because every Friday or Saturday night their parents would take them to the local video store (remember those?) as an event and wade through the latest video releases, which at the time were presented to us in bulgy cases sporting hideously graphic covers, in the same way that heavy metal album covers did: a great ploy to attract custom. At this time, many video cassettes were pre-certification.

Back in the early 1980s, VHS players (you remember, those now almost-extinct monsters which consumed video cassettes), and to a lesser extent Betamax players (which weighed a ton!), were a new thing and the video industry was booming. Although people loved going to the cinema to see the latest blockbuster, a lot of the films released weren't popular enough, or of sufficient budget, to make the big screen, and so families would go to the video store and hire out films for the weekend. (Oddly, one video shop my family were a member of also operated as a hair salon!) Remember as well that, back in those days, there were only a handful of channels on the television.

I was always a big horror fan, and we kids were spoilt for choice, even though we weren't exactly old enough to watch most of the films back then. Rumour was rife that certain films released at the time either a) showed scenes of real death and torture, or b) were considered so extreme in content that they were to be banned, or heavily censored. The trouble is, these rumours meant that people with a darkly curious eye were even more eager to snap up titles such as *The Texas Chainsaw Massacre*, *The Driller Killer*, *The Burning*, *The Evil Dead* and the like. The other problem was that people were recording these videos as what became known as 'pirate' copies, and would distribute them not just among friends and family, but also loan them out or sell them at local flea markets. In most cases the copies were of atrocious quality – and yet people still bought them! Mind you, it hasn't changed much with today's downloads.

Video nasties stirred up a great deal of controversy, and we were terrified that if we owned a horror film that was put on the video nasties list then our houses would get raided by the local police and our parents arrested. It's fair to say that some of the hype was justified, because certain films were excessively gory; and if you're going to make a film called *Snuff* then it's likely you will attract attention from the local fuzz, even if the film is nothing more than a low-budget horror. Ninety-nine per cent of the films out there were simply gory, nothing more, but the urban myths of the video nasty craze became so over-the-top that it seemed as if literally every film with an X certificate was vulnerable to being banned. Looking back I wonder what all the fuss was about, because many of the aforementioned films are now considered horror classics, and not the snuff films the urban legend suggested.

In 1982 several religious organisations, and campaigners such as Mary Whitehouse, called for stricter laws not just on video nasties but on certain heavy metal albums, which they believed were affecting the 'youth of today'. The British Board of Film Censorship was set up to monitor releases, and in 1984 the stricter Video Recordings Act was imposed. Again though, every time a film was put under scrutiny, more and more people were eager to view it and then distribute it within the local community. I remember, in my school, several boys passing around 'illegal' films that they had probably got from their older brother, and local markets were heaving with such videos. I recall several alleged raids and panic in the Medway Towns, in which videos were confiscated by police. I'm assuming the police had a list – although I'm guessing that they didn't in Manchester when a copy of Dolly Parton's film *The Best Little Whorehouse in Texas* was seized! Imagine the shock they got when they watched this tame film. The video nasty panic became so severe that several major news shows ran features, and I recall the next day at school talking to my mates in the playground about all the films the police had seized, and we spoke about which ones we'd seen or should see.

Films (especially those from the horror genre) didn't do themselves any favours in the 1980s, because the cover art was usually very graphic. When a video nasty list was put into action by authorities, it seemed that more than half of the films on the banned list were nothing more than low-budget thrillers which may or may not have included one mildly violent scene. But such was the uproar at the time that many movies were being tarred with the same brush. This is not to say that *some* films didn't show excessive violence.

When the popular television show *The Young Ones* aired an episode called 'Nasty' (which featured punk band The Damned singing a song called 'Video Nasty'), this was merely a reflection of the culture at the time – punk music and video nasties walked hand-in-hand as controversial siblings. It would take quite a few years for film censorship laws to loosen and enable classics such as *The Exorcist* the space to breathe and achieve the success they fully deserved. In the current climate, horror films are very much back in vogue, with films such as *Saw* depicting uncut graphic scenes of violence. However, some of the controversial films from the late 1970s and '80s, although released to the public, have been so heavily edited that they bear no resemblance to their official release.

I went to a few film fairs back in the 1980s and '90s and was amazed at the number of 'dodgy dealers' who would catch the eye of certain customers, and then, once the customer was close enough, produce a box of video nasties from under the table. Anyone would have thought the dealer was peddling drugs or dead bodies, such was the clandestine nature of it all. I also remember the *Daily Mail* starting a campaign in opposition to such films, because they believed that they were influencing children to become violent. In the modern climate, violent computer games are now considered the influential bogeyman. Of course, the other problem (and it was a major one) was the fact that once in a blue moon some maniac – apprehended for violent crimes – would blame a film for their dreadful acts. In the 1980s the *Daily Mirror* reported on the Kent horse-worrier who was accused of perpetrating a series of attacks on ponies. The newspaper stated that the assailant 'could be affected by video nasties or a new moon'. Panic indeed. Sadly, as recently as 1999, horror films were blamed when two boys were convicted of murder in Kent. Films such as *The Evil Dead* and *Scream* were cited by parents as a negative influence.

Back in the 1980s, lots of urban legends surrounded *The Exorcist* and *Poltergeist*. Both of these are considered classics that have stood the test of time, but many kids were more interested in the rumour that those involved in making the films had been dropping like flies. Some kids were so hysterical that they claimed if these films were watched a certain number of times then the viewer would die! I remember a lot of my friends talking about the hideous 'death mask' face said to pop up for a split second in *The Exorcist*. The legend was that if you watched the film in slow motion there were numerous subliminal messages and images. Watching *The Exorcist* in normal mode was a terrifying enough experience for many, so to spend hours watching it in slow motion in order to see some grotesque vision appear was insane. In the case of *Poltergeist*, many kids at school spoke of the actors and film crew who had died due to a curse, but this was nonsense. Even so, the film did give many children sleepless nights, especially the scene where a toy clown comes alive and accosts a child.

* * *

Another story going round school and local housing estates in the 1980s concerned a phantom hair clipper. You couldn't make this stuff up! Rumour had it that one night a young girl, who'd been out with some friends in Maidstone, had been walking home when she was accosted from the shadows by a madman who, with a pair of scissors or shears, snipped off a lock of her hair. The storyteller could not remember the girl's name or the exact location, but there certainly was a time when girls were frightened to walk home from school on those dark winter afternoons in case the hair-snipper took a chunk from their head. This urban legend may seem unique, but it isn't. In his book *Wild Talents*, Charles Fort – original chronicler of weird information – spoke of an incident that befell seventeen-year-old Doris Whiting. In the early 1900s, she was approaching her home at Orpington when she noticed a man leaning on the garden gate. According to Fort, 'As she was passing him, he grabbed her, and cut off her hair. The girl screamed, and her father and brother ran to her. They searched, but the clipper was unfindable [*sic*].'

In another case from Orpington, a maid employed at Crofton Hall was accosted by a hair-snipper who, having removed a chunk of her hair, simply vanished. Interestingly, the next incident returns to the fear of elevators, and the rumour that in the 1970s a rather unhinged character was frequenting the busy mechanical stairs at shopping malls, creeping up behind women, and cutting material from their flowing dresses in order to reveal their buttocks. I thought this urban legend was complete rubbish until I read of similar attacks taking place in London. The 'skirt slasher of Piccadilly' was the name given to this elusive snipper.

Phantom assailants have become popular in world folklore and have long been the stuff of urban legends. One of the funniest urban legends became known as The Phantom Sausage Slasher. The *Evening Post* of Friday 10 January 1969 reported on the 'Sausage slashers at work' after a local butcher shop was targeted by – wait for it – 'that mysterious band of men who specialise in banger bashing'! The shop hit was Kemsley's in Chatham High Street. Manager Mr P.G. Gordon commented to the press, 'Obviously the intruders were upset because there was nothing to steal, so they took their spite out on the sausages.' Urban legend gone mad, some would say.

Stabbers, slashers, hackers, flashers – you name it, there's an urban legend for it. During the 1830s in foggy London, some fifty years before the grisly reign of Jack the Ripper, there was said to exist a darkly clad individual known as Spring-Heeled Jack. This nocturnal terror was said to roam the cobbled streets of a night and wait in the shadows before leaping out upon unsuspecting women. The phantom – adorned in a cape and black hat (depending on where you read the story) – was said to breathe flames into the faces of his terrified victims, and then, with iron-like claws, slash away at their garments, usually to reveal their breasts. He would then laugh in sinister fashion and bound away at great heights – hence the name Spring-Heeled Jack. This odd character was also said to have caused panic in Surrey, Sussex and Kent, and became an urban legend for a short time, prowling the darkest corners of our imagination.

In Kent, Jack was said to have pounced upon a man and slashed him across his chest. At Keston, near Bromley, there was a vague report a few decades ago concerning three girls who were spooked by a cloaked figure, wearing a glowing belt, that seemed to glide over their heads. Despite becoming quite a potent legend, Spring-Heeled Jack appears to be nothing more than the sum of many different rumours. For instance, his visit to Sussex was described by *The Times* of 14 April 1838 as follows:

Spring-Heeled Jack has, it seems, found his way to the Sussex coast. On Friday evening, between nine and ten o'clock, he appeared, as we are informed, to a gardener near Rose Hill, 'in the shape of a bear or some other fur-footed animal,' and having first attracted attention by a growl, then mounted the garden wall, he ran along it upon all fours, to the great terror and consternation of the gardener, who began to think it time to escape.

He was accordingly about to leave the garden, when Spring-Heeled Jack leapt from the wall, and chased him for some time; the dog was called, but slunk away, apparently as much terrified as his master. Having amused himself for some time with the trembling gardener, Spring-Heeled Jack scaled the wall and made his exit.

It would seem, judging by this account, that Spring-Heeled Jack was either a fox, a domestic cat, or an escaped exotic cat from a private zoo – but nothing like the caped phantom we've come to know over the years.

✳ ✳ ✳

Another urban myth from the 1980s concerns a girl –
I won't give her name – from the school I went to. I think
it's fair to say that in most schools there are children who
wear nice clothes, and there are kids who aren't as fortunate;
there are children who are hygienic and those who aren't.
In some cases, children who weren't as hygienic were given
names such as 'stig', because their hair was unkempt and
their clothes were rarely washed. So, this girl rarely washed,
she always smelled bad and her hair was a hideous beehive.
According to some of the girls – at least those who were
brave enough to sit near her at school – she had insects living
in her hair. One girl, the playground gossip, claimed that a
big spider lived there. The Spider in the Hairdo is another
popular urban myth, and, whilst I'm sure this untidy girl may
not have washed her hair for a while, I doubt very much
that there were monstrous spiders and a menagerie of insects
residing in the knots and tresses. Another version of this
classic myth is that the person who has the awful hair keeps
a pet mouse in there. The more extreme version claims that
the girl in question eventually died because the spider and its
babies devoured her skull and munched on her brain!

In 1982, a boy from Harrietsham, in Maidstone, told
friends that an ant had burrowed into the ear of a friend of
his and began to munch on his brain. I had an ant go into
my ear when I was playing football one afternoon; the last
thing it wanted to do was crawl in further, and I imagine it
panicked more than I did – especially when I tipped fizzy
drink in my ear to flush it out!

Another hair story, from Oxfordshire, returns us to the
Devil. Allegedly, a lady from Eynsham took so long to do

her hair one Sunday that she arrived for Mass too late; as a punishment, the Devil descended upon her in the form of a spindly spider, and she died of fright. I am reminded of a hair-related and quirky urban legend that was passed down by my nan Win to my sister a few years ago. My nan said that you should never wash your hair on a Thursday during your menstrual cycle, as it will fall out!

If insects weren't the problem then it was germs. One girl I knew at infant school wasn't much of a looker, and a few of us annoying boys used to claim that she harboured love germs and that if you touched her accidentally they would rub off on you. I'm not quite sure what these love germs were but we always avoided her. If anyone was contaminated by these imaginary germs then they had to exorcise the contagion by grabbing it and blowing it away. There was another girl at school who rarely washed and was given the nickname 'Fleabag' by cruel kids. It was claimed that if you brushed past her then you would get fleas that stayed with you forever.

✳ ✳ ✳

Another weird bout of hysteria circulated around Kent when I was a child: bogus social workers. As if life wasn't scary enough with video nasties, playground gossip and terrors in the woods, reports were abundant concerning people posing as social workers who were knocking on doors and attempting to abduct children; this brings us once again to the bogus abduction scenario. The phenomenon, which became known as The Phantom Social Worker legend, became more popular in the early 1990s, but police investigations turned up no leads and no fake social workers were ever caught. In most cases, the groups who were rumoured to be carrying out the sinister operation consisted of several women and one man, who would keep their eye on a specific house and then knock on the door and claim that they were there to inspect the household after receiving a referral. According to legend, after the social workers had left, concerned parents would contact the police to report that the 'social workers' had attempted to remove, or at the very least examine, the children of the house. These scares echo similar cases of bogus electricians, gas fitters, policemen, etc., who are rumoured to enter households and rob occupants of possessions and money. Even as recently as 2012 there have been cases reported to the press regarding bogus social workers. No one seems to know if these people exist, or why they are never caught. In Issue 98 of *Fortean Times* magazine (May 1997), a list was drawn up of alleged bogus social worker appearances, but only one was said to have occurred in Kent; this was reported on 12 November 1996 in the Faversham area. The magazine commented that: 'A bogus doctor tricked her way into a disabled woman's house in Bysing Wood' and administered injections in both arms of the victim. Thankfully, the victim suffered no ill effects from the injections and was able to describe the mystery visitor as being in her thirties, with a pear-shaped face and brown, wavy hair. Oddly the incident, according to *Fortean Times*, 'was a re-enactment of a plot from the medical TV series *Dangerfield*'.

The majority of cases pertaining to the bogus social worker scare appear to originate from parts of the West Country. Two years previously, the same magazine had run an article by editor Bob Rickard on another bogus social worker. On one occasion in the North of England, a fake social worker left a house after failing to remove the child and then phoned the family, saying, 'You were lucky; next time I'll get your baby!'

Although in most cases tales of bogus social workers and the like are unfounded, over the last few years there have been reports in the press of bogus doctors being arrested in Kent, from Beckenham to Dover. One website claimed that 'fraudulent or rogue nurses' were being employed by up to 200 practices nationwide. It's no wonder such urban legends arise. My advice is: don't answer the door to anyone! And just when you thought it was safe to trust a policeman, another rumour which did the rounds at various Kent schools back in the 1980s was that a man, posing as a policeman, was attempting to entice children into his car. More recently, an issue of the *East Kent Mercury* ran the disturbing headline: 'Fake policeman jailed for targeting driver', after a lone female motorist travelling on the M20 at 4.30 a.m. was stopped by a vehicle with a flashing blue light. The man driving the vehicle asked the terrified woman to pull over and told her she was speeding. Only when the woman's brother and his friend came to her aid did the woman realise that the policeman was not all he seemed. The fake policeman was jailed for four months. In another case, reported in the *Evening Post* of 14 November 1969, the police were on the trail of a 'bogus meter man' who had been targeting properties in Sittingbourne and raiding gas and electric meters.

Nowadays it's not just the wolf that we have to keep from the door!

IF YOU GO DOWN TO THE WOODS (AND WATER) TODAY

... there are beasts everywhere.

✦

Danse Macabre, **Stephen King**

ANIMALS FEATURE QUITE heavily in urban legends. The Pet in the Oven, The Spider in the Hairdo and The Snake in the Blanket are well known, but the most popular American urban legend concerning animals is the long-lasting rumour that beneath the streets of New York City, in those dank, humid sewers, exist alligators. This fascinating urban legend has long been dismissed, despite several cases on record of such creatures being wrenched from their subterranean domain. Those who tell the stories of these out-of-place reptiles will have you believe that it was once quite popular for people to purchase baby alligators – possibly as pets for their children – and, as soon as the animals got too big or too expensive to feed, they were flushed down the toilet. In the early 1980s a horror flick called *Alligator* was released; it concerns a pet baby alligator which is discarded by its owners but grows to an enormous size and begins eating the locals. It was fun while it lasted, but no one took the legend seriously.

In the UK, when the animated children's show *Teenage Mutant Ninja Turtles* was at the height of its popularity, kids went crazy for them – to the extent that seeing the films and owning the toy figures wasn't enough. Parents purchased baby snapping turtles and terrapins as a novel pet, not considering that they were for life and not just for Christmas. Just like those baby alligators in New York, those pesky turtles were later dumped in local rivers, streams, lakes and ponds. These beasts were then seen basking in the sun at places such as Mote Park in Maidstone. Authorities claimed that cases were few and far between, until a massive snapping turtle turned up in a pond in Herne, and another in Faversham in 2010, and an alligator was found at Warden Bay on the Isle of Sheppey. The Faversham beast was the size of a dinner plate and was discovered by a vet in the vicinity of Oare; it was held responsible for the damage to the local eco-system for the last six years. The turtle, which is far removed from the characters of the cartoon series, is known for its bone-snapping jaws. Veterinary nurse Stacey Vangent bundled the creature into a dustbin after she spotted it sitting on a driveway.

On 10 January 2010, the *Telegraph* reported: 'Crocodile is living in a bungalow in Kent.' The spectacled caiman, named Caesar, was the pet of a retired civil servant named Chris Weller, from Strood. The newspaper also stated that some 4,296 wild animals were being kept across the country under the Dangerous Wild Animals licence. Animals in the list included wild boar, European lynx, various species of snake, lemurs, camels, antelopes, zebras, wolves and a red panda. It's no wonder that strange urban legends abound regarding sightings of animals in places they should not be.

The introduction of the 1976 Dangerous Wild Animals Act is the main reason why 'escaped animal' urban legends continue to circulate throughout the British Isles. Most of the snakes, and other exotic animals kept as pets, which escape or are released into the wild are recaptured, run over, shot dead or perish due to the climate. However, the UK has its own version of The Alligator in the Sewer legend; we call it Big Cats on the Loose.

When I used to visit Blue Bell Hill back in the early 1980s, I was more interested in the big cat that was supposedly on the loose than the rumour of a ghost or two. I'd always heard about these sightings but back then the legends were confined to the foggy moors of the West Country – an urban myth that locals called the 'beast of Exmoor'. Two decades previously there was the 'Surrey puma' of the 1960s – a large, sandy-coloured cat that no one could find evidence for, let alone capture. These stories soon spread across the fens, fields, woods and forests of England, and every county seemed to have a big cat legend, some of which remain to this day – although now we understand this mystery a little better. Or do we?

Big Cats on the Loose has pretty much taken over from the other urban legends us kids suffered many years ago. Nowadays a lot of people are hesitant to walk their dogs in the wilder local areas in case the big cat gets them, and parents continue to worry about the safety of their young children playing in the back garden of their semi-rural home. These stories are frequently covered in national and local newspapers, keen to get their 'beast of …' headline in there amongst the serious news reports. Such 'cat-flaps' (excuse the pun) usually come about when a frightened witness rings a newspaper to speak of their sighting, which in more cases than not will describe a 'Labrador-sized cat with a long tail', usually black or light brown in colour. During the 1960s, the 'Surrey puma' scare terrified people on the outskirts of leafy London because newspaper journalists and those who saw the animal didn't have much knowledge of cat species, and so as soon as reports filtered through to the Surrey-based newspapers of a 'sandy-coloured cat', headlines were quick to declare that a lioness was on the loose. Despite the comedy element, it didn't stop teams of police officers, RSPCA members, Scouts and housewives armed with rolling pins roaming the streets of Shooter's Hill looking for a lioness, which of course they failed to find. Sceptics argued that if there was a big cat on the loose then slaughtered livestock would be turning up, and there'd be paw prints dotted around the countryside. The problem was, people didn't know what signs they were looking for and that's the reason the 'Surrey puma' became an urban legend.

Down in glorious Kent there was no real headline-making 'big cat' story of the 1960s, '70s or '80s – the local press clearly weren't receiving the number of reports that Surrey or the West Country were. However, a resident of Cliffe named Leonard Cuckow knew all about the legends because he'd seen a big cat in Kent when he was a child – but this was in the 1930s! He was on the Burham Downs with friends, near Blue Bell Hill, when they observed an enormous black cat. They believed it had escaped from a local zoo and it was shot dead shortly afterwards by the Royal Engineers, or so they say.

This sighting never made the news because Leonard kept it to himself, until he told me around the late 1990s. The 'Surrey puma' and 'beast of Exmoor' were very much urban legends, tales passed around roaring log fires by farmers who claimed to have glimpsed the elusive beast. No one really believed them because no one could get a photograph – then again, these honest people, going about their daily grind, didn't expect to come upon such an animal whilst out tending to their flocks and fields.

In 1975 an incredible incident took place in Kent which involved an angler named Fred Lloyd, who was fishing on the banks of the River Medway at East Peckham. The story was covered by the *Daily Express* (7 January) and the *Weekly News* (18 January). The newspapers stated that Mr Lloyd had got the shock of his life when he heard a rustling in the bushes behind him. Suddenly a black animal, measuring around 2ft in length, tumbled down the bank. Instinctively, Mr Lloyd grabbed the animal by the scruff of the neck and then realised it was a panther, an animal which originates from the forests of Africa and Asia. As the animal growled and hissed, Mr Lloyd bundled it into his fishing box and rushed home, where he transferred the agitated felid to a playpen – which it demolished with haste. Mr Lloyd told the press, 'I phoned all the zoos I could think of to see if they had lost a black panther, but they just laughed at me and put the phone down.'

Not until twenty-four hours later did an RSPCA inspector arrive, and the cat was taken to a home in Surrey. Over a week later, Colchester Zoo in Essex claimed that an eight-week-old panther cub named Zar – worth around £600 – had been stolen from them on 4 January and they believed that the animal Mr Lloyd had caught was their own, although this was never verified. The place where Mr Lloyd had caught the cat was more than fifty miles from Colchester! So how on earth had the cat, if it really was the same animal, ended up in Kent?

Now, as I previously stated, the reason that alligators allegedly lurk in the New York sewers is that they were purchased as pets and then dumped. The same legend applies to the so-called big cats which seem to be thriving in our woods today. It is a known fact that, from the 1960s, to purchase a large exotic cat – or a cute and cuddly exotic cub – was quite commonplace, especially among the rich and famous (and the reckless) who were quite happy to walk into their local pub, or stroll down their street, with their pet leopard or lion in tow. So many people across England owned exotic cats as pets that by 1976 the Dangerous Wild

Animals Act was deemed necessary, and was introduced by the government as a way of controlling these bizarre purchases. Many exotic animals, from snakes and monkeys to large cats, were purchased from places such as Harrods, a large department store in London, but the majority of animals in England were bought via the black market. A chap from Orpington told me in 2010 that when he was a child in the 1940s, his dad would often go abroad for work and return with gifts for him. The man told me:

> On one occasion however dad brought back a rather strange looking small but stocky black cat which he said we could have as a pet … but it ate the next door neighbour's domestic cat! We didn't know what the cat was so my dad called a vet in who said it was a black leopard cub! My dad told me I couldn't keep it and so he went to the deepest woods in Kent that he knew of and released it.

When the 1976 bill was enforced, a lot of people tried to give their 'pets' to zoo parks, but these establishments could not always cope with the demand, and instead of having their novel pets destroyed the owners went for the easiest option and released them. The reason Big Cats on the Loose has become an urban legend is simply because there appears to be no solid evidence to back up these illegal releases; but then again, if you had a big cat in your collection back then and released it into the local forest, would you tell anyone?

Some people who owned exotic cats would not even have spoken about their pets, and kept them in cages in their back gardens, or in the basement of their house. Not only was this cruel – a large cat needs its territory – but these animals required large quantities of meat and were far more aggressive than your average guard dog. The strange, sleek, light-brown animal roaming Surrey in the 1960s was, if the sightings were genuine, almost certainly a puma (also known as cougar or mountain lion) that had escaped or been released. The fact that sightings were so scarce, and evidence almost non-existent, was perhaps down to the fact that a puma is an incredibly elusive animal, with a huge territory of hundreds of square miles. Such an animal mainly hunts at night, preferring to feast on rabbits, birds and rodents, as well as the occasional deer, rather than livestock. In the wild, they live only a few years beyond a decade, so how come people are still seeing the Surrey puma today?

What seems to have happened is that during the 1970s and early '80s, pumas, black leopards, and possibly lynx (once native to the UK) were released in small numbers across the countryside. There must have been sufficient numbers of each species to breed, because the animals people witness today are surely their offspring. Mind you, the newspapers at the time thought that one solitary, arthritis-ridden, grey old cat was roaming the whole of the British Isles for a century! These stories have become urban legends and a seemingly modern mystery. However, this is not a modern mystery. The press have only shown a keen interest in the sightings since the 1960s, a time when people owned such animals, but there are reports – such as the case of Leonard Cuckow from the Blue Bell Hill area – of animals being seen not just a few years previously, but many decades, if not centuries. During the Victorian era, travelling menageries and private collections existed in abundance and there are records which show that there were releases and escapes of numerous strange exotic animals. Some of these could have easily established themselves in the wilds of England – there is certainly enough prey and cover for a large elusive cat or two. There are reports of a strange animal roaming Surrey dating back to the nineteenth century.

In the modern age, researchers such as me are showing that there is abundant evidence to prove that such cats are not mere legend. Scat (faeces), paw prints, sheep/deer kills, hair samples and the like have been collated; carcasses of such cats are scant, but this is understandable when you consider how elusive the animals are. It seems that the presence of big cats in the UK will be classed as urban legend until some governing body admits otherwise, which seems unlikely. The ramifications of this admittance could be costly. For now, the animals are mere whispers on the wind, fleeting shadows in the mist, a bogey or spectre we cannot catch or even photograph. We love the mystery of it all, and we love telling the stories about how a friend of a friend of ours saw one on a dark night as they were driving along a remote back road. However, what must be made clear is that the only actual big cat rumoured to exist in Britain is the darker form of the leopard; lions, tigers, cheetahs and jaguars do not roam our wilds, despite the occasional press release. Meanwhile, the puma is the largest of the lesser cats, and not officially a big cat; in other cases, people are seeing smaller animals: the leopard cat, the jungle cat – animals which have actually been run over and shot dead.

To some, the thought of a big cat roaming our neighbourhood is something akin to the Loch Ness monster, but it's not comparable. There are real reasons why there are large cats prowling the woods, but it seems that no one is ready for these urban legends to come to life, so it's always a case of, 'Oh, I knew someone who knew someone that had a big cat and they let it go …'

* * *

Sightings of big cats have, for many years, been deemed the product of hallucination, or the result of a witness spending too much time in the local pub. Such beasts in our midst echo another urban legend, the lore of the Black Dog – also known as the hellhound. Urban legend states that if you ever see a giant black, spectral dog, then someone in your family will die. Another version of the legend is that you must not, despite temptation, stare into the eyes of the hellhound, for you will be turned to stone or cursed. Some folklorists believe that the modern-day sightings of big, black cats, with eyes that seem to glow, are current interpretations of hellhounds: salivating guardians of Hell that sporadically step into our timeframe. So-called big cats and Black Dogs are not the same, despite both being relegated to folklore. Hellhounds are most certainly urban legend – fiendish creations that exist in the same realm as ghosts, UFOs, goblins, fairies and the like. Black Dogs are just like the bogeyman – they follow weary travellers on country lanes of a night, but they can appear and disappear in the blink of an eye, or burst into flame. Some are reported as having no head, or dragging heavy chains around their neck, and in most cases these creepy canids are considered a bad omen. They are something akin to walking into the Grim Reaper on a stormy night.

Around the dark woods of Trottiscliffe in Kent there has long been rumour of a phantom hound, a creature sighted centuries ago and once known as the 'Great Dogge of the Pilgrims' Way'. One of the earliest records of this terrible beast comes from the year 1654, when it was said that a man walking on the 'upper road' of the Pilgrims' Way was frightened to death by the menacing hound. Maybe he stared at it for too long. The incident brings to mind the fictional hellhound written about in Sir Arthur Conan Doyle's *The Hound of the Baskervilles*.

Like the mythical dragon, the Black Dog has embedded itself into our folklore. They are creatures cast from the Ark to forever exist in some menagerie of the damned. They become urban legends because people fear them, and, because people spread rumours of their existence, they loiter in the back of our minds; and maybe, just maybe, on certain nights when the moon is full they are able to clamber out of our cranium onto that pathway.

A friend of mine named Paul Langridge told me about a very unsettling incident concerning his friend Mr Bitton, who one night in the 1980s was walking through Ranscombe Farm, a wooded area near the village of Cuxton near Strood, to see his friend Dave. Whilst walking along a woodland path, he became aware of the presence of an approaching dog, which began to accompany him on his journey. Even in the darkness Mr Bitton could see that it was large and brown in colour. There were farm dogs in the area but this dog appeared somewhat unusual. The dog displayed no emotion or reaction towards the witness, who stated that the oddest thing about the creature was the fact that when he put his hand out, the dog seemed to shift sideways. This movement was not of the dog's own doing; it seemed to be caused by Mr Bitton's outstretched hand, and, when he pulled his hand back, the dog would mysteriously 'pull' back towards him. The beast seemed to be some kind of surreal hologram.

After a short while, Mr Bitton was shocked to see the dog suddenly disappear. Many years later, after looking into legends of phantom dogs, Mr Bitton came to the conclusion that although the dog had expressed no malevolence, it was a harbinger of doom because, shortly after the sighting, Mr Bitton's friend Dave, whilst on holiday in Spain, crossed a road and was flattened by a lorry.

The British Isles boasts several well-known Black Dog legends, which are known by names such as Padfoot, Black Shuck, Barguest, Stryker and Guytrash. Lesser-known UK hellhounds are known as Hairy Jack, Churchyard Beast, Shug Monkey, Cu Sith, Galleytrot, Capelthwaite, Mauthe Doog, Hateful Thing, Swooning Shadow, Bogey Beast, Gurt Dog, and Catalan Dip – although, these phantoms could encompass several other mysteries and hauntings. Black Shuck (or Old Shuck) is a shaggy-haired spectral dog said to roam the coastline of Suffolk, Essex and Norfolk. East Anglian folk have spoken for centuries of this beast; in fact, its name possibly originates from the Anglo-Saxon term *scucca*, meaning 'demon'.

Legends of ghastly black hounds with eyes like burning coals are most certainly rife across the British Isles. However, Kent also boasts several peculiar and modern encounters with white hellhounds, the most fascinating coming, once again, from haunted Blue Bell Hill. Near the same stretch of hill said to be haunted by the phantom hitch-hiker, a phantom white dog was encountered on a cold and blustery November night back in 2001 by motorist Rick Flynn, who was coming from the direction of the Lower Bell public house. Suddenly, up ahead, he noticed a large white dog glide across the road. Mr Flynn braked hard to avoid it but the driver in the vehicle coming down the hill clearly didn't see the wraith as it slipped through the crash barrier and vanished. A few years before this, a calf-sized white creature was seen in the ancient village of Dode. A man staying in a cottage spotted the enormous, ghostly creature whilst looking out of the window. He noted how, in just a few seconds, the monster cleared a large field and all the rabbits in the vicinity scattered.

White spectral hounds have also been sighted on a dark road which leads out of Bluewater, the shopping centre at Greenhithe. In September 2006, at 1 a.m., a Mrs Whitmore and her husband were driving from Bluewater onto the slip road to the A2 when they both noticed a large, white, wolf-like creature on the road up ahead. The animal crossed the road slowly and arrogantly and, as the vehicle approached, the beast glanced back at the shocked couple. Mrs Whitmore said:

> It was not a cat or a dog but something resembling a wolf only stockier and bigger and whitish-grey in colour. The animal had a snout like a German Shepherd dog and large pointed ears, one of which was darker in colour than the other.

The couple were so unnerved that they drove off. On 25 May 2007, at 2.30 a.m., a motorist named Zoe was travelling on the same dark stretch of road when suddenly she 'missed a large white canine which looked like a wolf or a husky dog and as large'. She could see another one in the distance. Zoe swerved to avoid the animal, almost running her car into a roadside ditch. She stopped the car and her friend, who had been in the car behind, came to her aid. Bizarrely, Zoe's friend saw no dogs in the road.

Two phantom hounds are said to haunt Leeds Castle in Maidstone. One is a large black hound which has embedded itself in local legend, whilst the other is a small white ghost dog resembling a terrier. These are possibly the ghosts of deceased pets which once resided at the place. Mind you, the urban legend concerning the Black Dog of the castle has been doing the rounds for several centuries – from the time of Henry VI. It is claimed that in a certain room of the castle, the Duchess of Gloucester practised the dark arts and may well have summoned the apparition of the Black Dog. Details differ, but most storytellers agree that the Black Dog of Leeds Castle might be a good omen rather than one of malevolence. This is due to the fact that, many years ago, a member of the Wykeham-Martin family (who resided at the castle prior to the First World War) was sitting at a bay window in the Queen's Room, overlooking the moat, when they observed a dark-coloured dog in the room. Feeling no negativity from the spirit, they got up from their seating position and walked towards the animal to stroke it, whereupon it vanished. Seconds later, the bay window where they had been sitting cracked and crumbled into the waters below. It was as if the ghostly dog had saved them.

This urban legend may have been adapted from a more mundane event. James Wentworth Day wrote that, one night, two sisters had a terrible dream concerning their brother, General Martin of Gibraltar. In this dream – or should that be nightmare? – the girls saw the bay window, where their brother often snoozed, crumble into the moat below. In the morning, they removed his bedding from the sill and placed it elsewhere in the room. When General Martin bedded down for the night in another corner, the bay window did indeed collapse; the dream his sisters had experienced most certainly saved his life. Where the legend of the Black Dog came from we'll never know, but it has proven to be a rather atmospheric addition to this myth.

Reports of phantom hounds also emerge from the Isle of Sheppey. Shurland Hall is said to have several strange legends attached to it, one concerning the spectre of a big, black dog. Cranbrook's Skull's Gate Farm is also reputedly haunted by a hound – a long-bodied ghost dog with the facial features of a human. This urban legend has been passed down over a century or so and is based on a murder that allegedly took place in the late nineteenth century. The spectral dog's human face is said to be that of the murdered man. Chronicler Charles Igglesden wrote of the hideous legend in *A Saunter through Kent with Pen and Pencil*, stating that the most recent sighting (in the early 1900s) he'd heard of concerned a man who encountered the vile manifestation while riding his bicycle. Stay away from Skull's Gate Farm – the name of the area alone sounds petrifying! There is a legend of another man-faced hound from Tenterden, in an area known as The Wood Way.

* * *

Whether people actually see phantom hounds is difficult to say, but many reports of strange creatures, real or otherwise, are passed down as urban legend. One urban legend I always found creepy as a child was said to have taken place somewhere in East Kent in the 1970s. It concerned a young boy who kept a large snake – possibly a boa constrictor – as a pet. According to a friend of a friend who knew the boy, many a night, when the boy was asleep, the pet snake would lie alongside him. His parents, who had bought the creature, thought this rather cute and assumed that the snake was attempting to gain warmth from his body. However, according to the friend of a friend, the snake was in fact sizing up the boy and planning to eat him! Another version states that the snake crushed the boy to death. I've heard this tale many times before, and it has echoes of the popular American urban legend known as The Snake in the Blanket, in which an escaped snake coils up in a pile of clothing, much to the alarm of the person who finds it. An alternative version is that a snake, coiled up in a crate of fruit that has been imported from abroad, bites someone in a store. Although this version has become classic urban legend material, snakes genuinely have turned up on quite a few occasions in fruit crates, and in Kent. In most cases, snakes found curled up in rugs, or under floorboards, have either escaped their tank or are from a pet shop. Most will die due to the climate. Another version of The Snake in the Blanket legend is that a snake finds itself curled up in a warm and cosy place – e.g. a roll of carpet in a shop or a pile of clothes – and remains undisturbed for so long that it produces young, and the next minute the location is swarming with slithering snakes. The local community then has a snake plague to deal with!

One of my favourite Kentish snake stories comes from the pages of *The Public Ledger* of 19 July 1842. The headline ran: 'A Boa Constrictor At Large In England.' Here is an extract from the article:

> A boy in the service of Mr Grange, Willgrove, Kent, who was employed in tending sheep on the waste lands bordering on a rather extensive tract of woodlands, known as the Fells, came running in a state of breathless haste and alarm to the residence of his master, and gave the following extraordinary account: He was lying on the ground, he said – watching the sheep, near to the hedge that separates the wood from the waste, when his attention was attracted by hearing a crackling noise in the hedge, and immediately afterwards a large snake darted out, and made a spring at one of the lambs.

According to the boy, the lamb escaped from the snake, which he thought measured between 10ft and 15ft. Mr Grange, rather sceptical of the story, went to investigate and found the large specimen wrapped around a tree. The creature was eventually shot by Mr Grange, who sought aid from two men. When measured, the snake was said to be 6ft 4in in length, with a girth of 1ft. Rumour has it that the snake escaped from a travelling zoo which had been stationed some two miles away the previous night.

In 1968 it was reported that hordes of killer snakes were inhabiting the undergrowth on the outskirts of Chatham's Weeds Wood Estate. The *Evening Post* of 27 August ran the shocking headline: 'Snake threat to children', after it was claimed that a youngster had been bitten by an adder. The hysteria, and risk, died down when children stopped cornering the unfortunate snakes, which were all too eager to flee rather than attack.

Two years later, people in Gillingham began spreading rumours that a monster lizard was on the loose. Gillingham police commented at the time that he 'could be dangerous', even though the creature turned out to be a 3ft-long hooded South American iguana that had escaped the van of a pet-shop owner from Canterbury Street in Gillingham. Sadly, the monster story fizzled out quickly.

The *Chatham Standard* of 6 September 1988 reported: 'Python still eludes owners', describing a 5ft-long creature that had escaped in Wigmore. Coincidentally, as I'm assuming it wasn't the same beast, the 27 September edition refers to a young boy finding an 8ft-long python near Berengrave Nursery not far from Wigmore.

One of the oldest snake urban legends in Kent concerns the Isle of Thanet. Although no longer an island, the place is said to be completely bereft of snakes (a good thing, some might say!). Legend has it that St Augustine drove every snake from the isle and cursed them forever. St Isidore of Seville (560-636) recorded: 'It is named Thanet (tanatos) from the death of serpents. Although the island itself is unacquainted with serpents, if soil from it is carried away and brought to any other nation, it kills snakes there.'

In most cases, the actual monster of the piece in an urban legend is the person who's telling the story. He or she can add or subtract details depending on what they know or don't know. They can fit the legend in with the current climate and exaggerate the twist or the bogeyman to suit their own fears and beliefs. During this process, there's a good chance that the original facts of the story – if there were any in the first place – are stretched considerably.

* * *

Centuries ago, sailors who travelled across the foaming oceans of the world spoke of seeing mermaids. These sirens were figures of misfortune, who sat atop rocks combing their hair, enticing sailors overboard to their watery death. In other versions, the mermaids caused boats to collide with jagged rocks hidden beneath the frothing waves. Of course, mermaids don't exist – or do they?

Well, a fair few years ago, maybe around 1991-2, a friend of mine named Steve R. came up to me in the pub and said that a mate of his, who knew someone who worked behind the bar (yep, it's another friend-of-a-friend tale!), knew someone who used to work in a pub that had an actual mermaid in a glass case. I had to laugh when I heard this. The story goes that many years ago a relative of this person came into possession of a hideous exhibit said to have been captured out at sea sometime during the nineteenth century. Apparently the creature was a shrivelled mermaid that had been caught in a fishing net – goodness knows where – and was taken aboard the boat, where it had died. It was then put in a glass case as a gruesome exhibit. Now, I was engrossed by this story, mainly because it echoed a similar tale from the 1800s when a Captain Eades had purchased a mermaid from a sailor abroad and exhibited it in London. Eventually, much to the dismay of Captain Eades, the beast turned out to be a hoax, a weird combination of wire, fish tail and monkey torso.

My friend was adamant that his story was true. 'But how can it be?' I asked. 'Mermaids don't exist.' And that was where the story ended. Until …

A couple of years ago, I was trawling through some newspaper archives when, to my amazement, I came across the following snippet: 'Real wonders! At Gravesend', and a story of a weird exhibition dating back to August 1825, but not recorded in print until 1890:

A Gravesender visited these wonders in company with his children, and saw the mermaid, which he says, 'was about 2-ft high and had one arm – the other having been cut off and sold. The woman who exhibited it, declared to me it was no imposition, that it had been inspected, very minutely in London, by professional gentlemen and that it was pronounced to be a mermaid.

What a wonderful story, I thought. It brought to mind another Kentish mermaid tale I heard just after I left school in the early 1990s. This concerned an elderly lady who lived 'somewhere' in Medway, who apparently, many years ago, had been given the hand of a mermaid by a merchant seaman – who knows, maybe it was the hand severed from the Gravesend specimen. According to the legend, the limb had magic powers, and it was said that if you owned the mermaid's hand you would be granted three wishes. I would have loved to believe this story but I was all too familiar with the classic W.W. Jacobs horror story *The Monkey's Paw*, from 1902. In this fictional tale, Mr and Mrs White are given a shrivelled monkey's paw as a gift by a friend, Sergeant-Major Morris, who tells them he has no use for the item but that it has special powers. Sergeant-Major Morris warns the Whites to be very careful what they wish for, and so, Mr White wishes for £200 to put forward as a final payment for his house. Sadly, there is a gloomy twist, because although the Whites get their money, it comes at a terrible cost. Their son, Herbert, has an awful accident at work and is mutilated – resulting in his death. The family receive £200 compensation for this.

After the funeral, Mrs White, consumed by grief, begs her husband to use the paw to wish that their son can return, and reluctantly Mr White makes the wish. After a short while there seems to be a presence outside the front door, and Mrs White fumbles at the lock, believing it to be Herbert back from the dead. But Mr White, who saw the corpse of his son and the terrible extent of his injuries, realises that the man outside the door will not resemble Herbert, but will appear as something much more horrific. So Mr White grabs the monkey's paw and wishes his son away. Mrs White opens the front door but there is no one there. Chilling.

The moral of this story is to not mess with fate.

＊ ＊ ＊

Anyway, back to the saga of the Kentish mermaid. So there I was, many years later, still trawling through newspaper archives hoping to come across some quirky or weird stories, when I flicked through a copy of the *Evening Post* of 8 January 1969 and saw a grotesque, yet eye-catching, sight. There, in black and white, was a photograph of a hideous creature deemed to be a mermaid – and a Kent one at that. So, my friend's legend had been right – partly anyway. The small article stated: 'If you believe in mermaids, this gruesome skeleton could mean you're right.' The photograph had been submitted by a Mr Peter Denne of Canterbury Street, Gillingham. He claimed that the mermaid had been photographed by his father Albert more than thirty years previously, when he was in the Royal Navy venturing to the South Sea Islands. According to the legend, the mysterious beast had floated to the surface of the ocean after being dislodged by a depth charge.

In the *Evening Post* of 13 January 1969, another ghastly image appeared. The headline read: 'The thing shows signs of life, says Gus.' Mr Gus Britton, landlord of the Cannon public house at Brompton, had produced another mermaid. He stated that he'd taken this macabre exhibit to Rochester Museum and the Natural History Museum for analysis, and, whilst experts all agreed it was a weird fake, none could determine what creatures made up the grotesque mermaid. Now, I've collected stories about unusual Kentish legends for many years, but to see them backed up by such bizarre photos was a joy. The fiendish critter seemed to provoke a decent response from the public because, on 21 January 1969, a C.R. Taylor of Strood wrote:

I saw one of these creatures in Gillingham Park more than forty years ago. The head was partly covered by wisps of red hair. The teeth were pointed and the eye sockets very round. It was rather repulsive and if I remember correctly about 20 inches long. Definitely not a subject for sailors to dream about. This strange creature was on show at a park fete about the middle 1920s. It was lent by the owner of a small private collection living in Mill Road, Gillingham.

The following week another letter appeared in the newspaper under the heading: 'Man-Fish Is A Man-Hoax.' Ian G. Tubby wrote: 'That man-fish you featured is a hoax I'm afraid to say. I was told many years ago in the Merchant Navy that these were made as curiosities by the Chinese in Shanghai about 1920-30 and sold to tourists. Most were bought by sailors, it seems!' The letter concluded that such 'mermaids' were in fact constructed from the parts of a small monkey (usually the head and torso) and the tail of a large fish such as a carp. This was confirmed in a letter written by Fred Sanders of Sydney Road, Chatham, printed in the newspaper on 3 February: 'It's a bit of monkey business … The Japanese are presumed first to have manufactured them. Others came from China and East Indies. The earliest specimen was recorded from 1813 from the island of Saint Helena.' Sanders also mentioned the mermaid that was paraded around London in the 1820s, and concluded: 'A good many years ago an old Chatham public house had one on display in the public bar. There has been mention of others in the Medway Towns over the past 150 years.'

This was to be the last mention of the Kentish mermaid legend, although, rather fittingly, two days later the newspaper covered the story of a shrunken head kept by a Rochester woman named Joyce Keam. She stated that the item had been passed down by her father, who had housed it in his private museum after receiving it from an Amazonian tribe.

So, the urban legend of the local mermaid wasn't complete fiction after all, and, maybe in the case of similar urban myths, there's a truth to be found … somewhere. This certainly seems to be the case with the legend that I like to call The Medway Serpent, or, Don't Run Across the Bridge or the Monster Will Get You.

I once heard of an urban legend concerning a monstrous creature said to inhabit the waters of the River Medway. The Medway winds for some seventy miles; its silted waters flow through Kent, but the river begins just inside the West Sussex border and enters the Thames Estuary. I heard that if you creep across the Rochester Bridge, which runs from Rochester to Strood, then the local serpent won't hear you and you'll be safe, but if it hears the patter of feet it will rise out of the water and snap you up. This sounds like something from a Japanese B-movie. However, I was contacted by a chap named Richard Mann, who told me matter-of-factly that as a child he always ran across the bridge, and the reason for this was because of what had happened quite a few years previously. One afternoon, he had descended the steps that used to lead to the civic centre, which is no longer there, when he saw a black, circular object in the water. Richard was rather curious and approached the water's edge to look down. Suddenly the object uncoiled and swam off like a giant black eel or snake, more than 30ft in length. He was so terrified that every time he crossed Rochester Bridge after this he would sprint, never once looking down at the grey water in case the beast was loitering there.

What an amazing story, I thought, but surely this was just an urban legend, something akin to the monster in the closet?

I was wrong. Although porpoise, seal, and sturgeon have turned up in the Medway over the years, it seems unlikely that some large, and I mean truly large, creature could live down there and evade detection. Even so, in 1947 some leviathan of the deep was pursued through the River Medway by a man named Jack Pocock. The classic fisherman's tale of The One That Got Away is something we've heard time and time again, but this time something very big did get away. Just.

Jack was aboard his boat in the vicinity of Sun Pier, Chatham. Suddenly, looking across the water, he noticed a greyish creature resembling a monstrous eel, measuring approximately 40ft in length. The creature had a strange, long snout and a humped back, which seemed to be lined with bristles. Jack's son Thomas arrived on the scene with a 12-bore shotgun, which he fired at the beast – but to no effect, and it disappeared without a trace. The next day Tom loaded his gun with ball bearings, and when it appeared once again he fired, causing the monster to shudder and then slip out of sight. After the second incident, people nationwide got to hear about the creature of the Medway. The animal, or whatever it was, was seen again a week later at Gillingham Reach. It appeared close to Tom Pocock's boat, and on this occasion the man's gun was equipped with 6in cartridges, used to bringing down big game. But the creature once more evaded its pursuers and was never seen again.

Had the urban legend come to life? Had Richard seen the same creature, or possibly one of its offspring, lurking beneath Rochester Bridge? In 2008 the *Medway Messenger* reported that several people residing in apartments along Rochester's Esplanade had observed an enormous humped creature swimming towards Strood Bridge. Maybe they had seen a porpoise, but we'll never really know. One thing is for sure: this was another urban legend with some element of truth attached. And, of course, sometimes big fish really do lose their way. In 1949 a narwhal arrived on the shore of the River Medway, the first in the country for more than 500 years. Sadly the creature died in the bay at Wouldham.

* * *

Monsters make for great urban legends. And it's not just giant fish or alligators in the sewers which make the headlines. Phantom kangaroos have been sighted for several decades across America, leaving witnesses bemused. The kangaroo is the largest living marsupial, native to Australia, and yet sightings persist elsewhere, making these animals the stuff of legend.

On 25 October 2005 the *Guardian* reported: 'Beast of Beckenham catches golfers on hop', after several sightings of an unusual animal at Beckenham Park. One golfer, about to take a swing on the green, fled the scene after seeing what he described as a kangaroo. The Natural History Museum examined a large footprint in the area but stated that the evidence was inconclusive. Later in 2005, a strange, hopping creature was hit by a car close to Lenham Storage Yard at rural Maidstone. The animal was killed instantly and further examination revealed that it was a wallaby. These marsupials, also native to Australia, were once housed in parks and on farms across the South East. Many ended up in the wild when what became known as the 'Great Storm' ripped through Kent in 1987, resulting in animals escaping their pens and cages. Wild boar also escaped into the woods, particularly in the Ashford/Canterbury and Sussex area. On 9 May 2012 a wallaby was filmed in the village of Pluckley (two months after one was run over on the Isle of Sheppey) by resident Alex Pooley. She was walking her dog, Shackleton, when the animal bounded towards them. Alex had the presence of mind to reach for her camera phone before it bounded away.

Those who investigate the big cat urban legends believe that the 1987 Kent storm was to blame for subsequent sightings of large cats, particularly in the East Kent area. On 13 October 1987, a local paper reported: 'Leopard and two monkeys escape cages', after the storm ripped through Howletts Zoo. The article continued: 'A snow leopard which escaped on Friday, after a tree crushed its cage, was still at large last night.' A similar incident spawned another legend a year later, when the local press reported: 'Escaped panther may have killed park animals', after 'a fawn, two dozen chickens and two ducks' were killed at Brambles Wildlife Park near Canterbury.

From rumour of exotic and deadly spiders being found at Chatham Docks, to reports of mink in their droves, a piranha in a pond at Folkestone, and tales of swordfish and sharks being caught off the Kent coast – and not forgetting the jackal shot in Sevenoaks in 1905 and the Hawkhurst bear of 1983 – Kent seems to be where the wild things are and a place where urban legends are born.

✳ ✳ ✳

When I was young, my granddad often told me that in faraway lands existed a peculiar exotic bird named the Oozlum bird. This elusive creature, according to my granddad, 'Often flew backwards but more so around in circles and in some cases it would disappear up its own backside.' This was a hilarious legend that echoed similar tales of animals that could not exist but which were reported across the world. Heronden, in Ashford, is said to get its name from a bird-related urban legend. Charles Igglesden, writing in the early 1900s, stated:

> It is said that the place derived its name from a family of Herons. This is probably the case, but I cannot refrain from giving an old legend connected with the place, and which, if true, might have caused the place to be called Heronden.
>
> Once upon a time – so the story goes – the tiny child of a woodcutter in Heronden Park was wont to play from daybreak to nightfall in an opening among the trees. Here, too, came herons in great number, and in the course of time would stand around the little girl, allowing her to stroke their downy feathers and place her arms around their tall thin legs. But one day a huge golden eagle swooped down upon the child, lifted her by its cruel beak and soared away into [the] distance. At the approach of the eagle the simple herons had vanished into the trees, but when they saw their little friend carried off, and heard her piteous cries, they rose in a body and gave chase to the thief. And they reached him just as he lay his victim on the ledge of a distant rock. He fought and struggled with his pursuers, but although many fell dead and wounded, the others persevered and conquered.
>
> When the woodcutter arrived he found his child caressing a heron, and at her feet lay the eyeless body of the dead eagle. And henceforth, adds the legend, the spot was called Heronden.

Another bird legend was told to me in the 1980s when I was at a family wedding reception in Chatham. A second cousin of mine told me that his friend, who was Italian, always threw rice at their family weddings instead of confetti, but, when the birds ate the rice, they exploded! There is, of course, not a shred of truth in this bizarre statement, but it does remind me of those people who used to say that they knew people who would insert a straw into the backside of a frog and then blow it, causing the frog to puff up and explode.

Birds are often portrayed as sinister in urban legends. I have several friends who are spooked by crows because they believe such creatures to be omens of death. I recall that one morning, as I was rousing from sleep, I heard a tapping on the bedroom window – rather odd, considering I lived about 60ft up in the air on a top-floor apartment. I looked at the window and to my astonishment saw a crow perched on the windowsill looking at me through the windowpane. The bird knocked a couple of times and then flew away. Crows feature heavily in tales of superstition, as does the magpie, but whatever irrational fears we have of them, they are simply birds and nothing more.

It was once rumoured that witches were accompanied by crow familiars; the creature, alongside the black cat, thus became an emblem for their alleged dark practices. In England, some people recite the following rhyme when they see a crow:

One is anger, two is mirth,
Three a wedding, four a birth,
Five is heaven, six is hell,
Seven is the Devil himself

Imagine my shock when I was walking in the vicinity of Hayes one day, not far from Bromley, when I looked down a cul-de-sac to see it covered by crows. I don't mean five or six, not even twenty; there were literally hundreds of them – so black that they smothered the road. I'm not sure what this sighting meant but I decided they were feeding on something in that area.

The crow's cawing is recognisable, but legend states that if you hear a hoarser sound emanating from the bird then it means bad weather is on the way. There is also a rhyme which relates to the magpie, although this sometimes gets confused with the rhyme that applies to the crow:

> One for sadness, two for mirth,
> Three for marriage, four for a birth,
> Five for laughing, six for crying,
> Seven for sickness, eight for dying,
> Nine for silver, ten for gold,
> Eleven for a secret that will never be told

Of course, these rhymes vary. The common two-line rhyme about the magpie is:

> One for sorrow, two for joy,
> Three for a girl, four for a boy.

Those who see a magpie often salute it, or, if it's morning, they say, 'Good morning Mr Magpie', as if not doing so will bring them bad luck. In some instances people ask the bird, 'How is your wife today?'

It seems rather strange that we salute a bird; maybe it's because the magpie, like the brazen fox of England, has a mischievous side that we fear. The creature roams into our towns and into our back gardens – and, if legends be believed, into our homes to steal our jewellery. Even the perfectly natural hoot of an owl sends a shiver down the spine.

Animals that prowl in the night have always instilled dread within us, and so maybe we salute and acknowledge them as a mark of respect. The cry of an owl has long been considered an omen of disaster, and, if heard close to a home, it promises a terrible life to any child about to be born. So many birds have weird legends attached to them. Legend has it that inside the stomach of a swallow two magical stones are carried – one of the stones, black in colour, is said to bring good luck, whilst a red stone cures madness. It is also said that the kingfisher got its marvellous colours of orange and blue because Noah sent one such bird out to search for dry land after the Flood, but it flew so high that the sun and sky tainted its wings. Many years ago, ravens were said to be the Devil's birds; and the sound of a curlew was once believed to be the warning from a drowned friend.

Countless rhymes, songs and traditions are born from our fear and love of animals; even insects have become part of urban legend. My mother finds it eerie if she finds a cricket in the home – many people believe that it is a sign of death but, as is the case with so many superstitions, this is simply down to interpretation.

I've also heard numerous urban legends about people owning ferocious animals in built-up areas. I'd like to have a few quid for every story passed down about 'a man who used to live up the road who owned a bear/lion'. One urban legend passed down over the years was that, in the 1980s, a man on the Isle of Sheppey owned a big cat which he kept in a cage in his garden. Allegedly, another man 'owned a couple of lions which he used to let walk around on top of his hotel balcony … he bought the lions to deter burglars'.

These are fantastic feline legends – and oddly, there is some fact to them. At least two people on the island owned lions, one in an area known as Blue Town. The beasts were kept in a trailer. However, it was the Big Cats in a Cage legend which stuck in my head as I was growing up. Most people I'd spoken to claimed that a big black cat had been released on the Isle of Sheppey and that it was probably the one kept in the cage. The animal kept in the cage was in fact a puma called Kitten. I'm unsure what happened to the cat but it was probably not released on the island. It is also a known fact that people used to drive slowly by the enclosure as the 'pet' gradually became a tourist attraction. I'd also been told as a child that lots of people kept bears as pets and, when I passed these stories on, people would scoff at the suggestion. However, I know of a handful of cases involving people who really did keep bears as pets; in one instance, a honey bear was kept as a pet on the Isle of Sheppey, and, according to the 31 October 1968 issue of the *Evening Post*, a pet Himalayan black bear was kept at a smallholding at Bearsted in Maidstone. The animal was owned by the Lunnons, and mauled the Lunnons' daughter, Barbara, when she put her arm through the bars of the cage. Barbara's arm was amputated.

Sheppey has another animal urban legend, dating back to the fourteenth century, which has become known as Grey Dolphin. Robert de Shurland, who resided at the reputedly haunted Shurland Hall, allegedly killed a monk and was pursued across the land by the local sheriff. He rode on horseback to the King in order to seek forgiveness. After he had been pardoned, he began his journey back home. However, en route he bumped into a local witch who told him that his own horse – named Grey Dolphin – would be the death of him. Robert initially scoffed at the remark, but quickly became perturbed by the warning and so decided to kill his horse and decapitate it.

A year or so later, de Shurland had forgotten all about the grisly act he had committed on his horse, and also the warning from the witch. But whilst walking along the shore one day he trod on a bone which punctured his foot. Blood poisoning set in and eventually killed him. The bone had belonged to Grey Dolphin. In a slightly different version of the legend, it is said that a year after killing his horse, Robert was walking along the beach when he stumbled across the skull of the animal. So enraged was he that he kicked it; one of its teeth penetrated his boot and pierced the sole of his foot, and from that injury came his death.

On a lighter note, I once heard from a school friend that blue-headed swans had been observed in the River Medway and were considered a bad omen. Interestingly, this was the same guy who told me about the mermaids, and whilst that proved to be true – to some extent – blue-headed swans were just laughable. My friend told me that the story had been passed to him from his mum, and so for me, this was another urban myth. Until, that is, I came across the 27 June 1969 edition of the *Evening Post*. I was flabbergasted when I saw an article on blue-headed swans in the River Medway. However, these were not freaks of nature; there was a more prosaic explanation. According to the newspaper:

> A strange looking swan with a blue head and bright yellow feet has been spotted paddling up the River Medway, but alas, for bird watchers this is no rare ornithological find – just one of the twelve survivors of February's oil pollution which wiped out the majority of the local swan population.

One final urban legend regarding swans concerns the rare black variety, which reside on the waters around Leeds Castle. It is said that if these swans ever leave the castle then tragedy will befall the place. This echoes a similar legend from Closeburn Castle in Scotland, where such beautiful creatures were considered omens of good luck until one was shot with an arrow. From then on, it was said that every time a red-breasted swan appeared at the castle, a member of the Kirkpatrick family would die.

MORE STRANGE URBAN LEGENDS

All the teller really has to do is to keep the catalogue of inexplicable events in their correct order, so that unease escalates into outright fear.

◆

Danse Macabre, Stephen King

'If you eat an apple pip a tree will grow inside your stomach.'

'If you swallow chewing gum it wraps around your intestines and kills you.'

'If you swallow chewing gum it can stay in your system for more than seven years.'

'If you swallow an orange pip you will get appendicitis.'

'If you see a frog in the road it means you will come into some money.'

'If a bride sees birds in flight, she has chosen Mr Right.'

'If you buy a horse with one, two or three white legs it means bad luck.'

'If you see bats, it's a sign of scandal.'

'Bats get tangled up in your hair.'

'If you stare into a mirror too long you start to feel woozy and your face deforms; sometimes it turns into a demon.'

'Whilst sleeping at least seventeen spiders will crawl into your mouth … each year.'

'If a woman is pregnant she is allowed to urinate in a policeman's hat.'

'If you swim directly after you've eaten a meal you will die.'

These are just a handful of examples of urban legends and old wives' tales passed down over the years. Despite the dramatic nature of such statements, none of them are true. If you swallow an apple or orange pip nothing will happen. Chewing gum will most definitely not wrap itself around your insides and take over your body – although it's never advisable to swallow something that isn't meant to be swallowed. The digestive system can't break down gum like it can most other foods, but eventually the gum will be passed through the intestine and out of your rear end!

If you see a frog in the road it will probably get run over – unless you can rescue it. But be careful that you too don't get hit by a car. Birds in flight mean nothing at all to a bride, just be careful they don't excrete on that lovely wedding dress. A horse with three white legs is not a problem – just make sure it has a fourth leg, otherwise it'll make for a terrible racehorse. As for those pesky bats, you'll be lucky to see one in the dead of night. Although they have relatively poor eyesight, they use sonar to detect their prey. There is no reason for a bat to get tangled in someone's hair – except in a horror film. Bats feed off small insects, so if you haven't washed your hair for many years and an abundance of insects reside there, then watch out! If you stare into a mirror for too long your friends and family will desert you for being a loner and consumed by vanity. If a spider crawls into your mouth whilst you're sleeping you'd probably feel it, but if not, what's it going to do – eat the chewing gum out of your stomach? According to some websites, it is fine for a woman to request she borrow a policeman's helmet to empty her bladder – but finding a policeman on the streets of Kent today is nigh on impossible, so buy your own novelty helmet! And lastly, eating a big meal and then jumping into the pool for a swim could cause cramps, but death will only occur if you choke to death … on the spider you had the night before. We could go on forever with these stories. And now for a few more Kentish legends that have been doing the rounds.

✧ 'Footballer paid our mortgage' ✧

In May 2012 I was at the house of a friend of mine, watching the FA Cup Final between Liverpool and Chelsea. We were discussing the extortionate wages that footballers get and the arrogance of some players, when my friend's partner said: 'Friends of ours were telling us that their friends wanted to get married at Cooling Castle [near Rochester] but were phoned by the castle, who told them that the date they had booked for their wedding eighteen months in advance was being opposed by an anonymous footballer. Apparently the footballer, who plays for Chelsea, wanted the same date and said he'd do whatever it took to book the date he wanted.'

I listened intently, taken in by the story, wondering who the mystery footballer might be. My friend's girlfriend added: 'The footballer told the manager of the castle that he was willing to pay for the couple's wedding if they moved the date, but they said no. A few days later they got another call from the castle manager saying that the footballer was now willing to pay the couple's mortgage off just so he could use that specific date, and they agreed. A few weeks later the couple received a cheque, signed by a famous footballer.'

Naturally, I found this a rather interesting story; my friends' friends believed that the player might have been someone like Chelsea midfielder Frank Lampard, although there was also a rumour that the anonymous footballer was simply booking the date – out of sheer arrogance – to stop anyone else using it. I found this most odd, and my suspicions were confirmed when later in May I was in a bar in Rochester and overheard a group of customers telling the same story. A quick bit of research revealed that this tale is a modern urban legend, and when it originated it was said to concern famous footballer David Beckham. In April 2012, several newspapers ran features stating: 'Christine Bleakley denies claims she and Frank Lampard bribed two couples to give up their wedding venues.' Apparently, a source close to the pair told the *Sun*: 'All these tales are just an urban myth. The same rumours circulated when David and Victoria Beckham announced they were to wed.'

✧ *The Crying Boy* ✧

When I was young, my mum and dad owned a picture called *The Crying Boy*. This mass-produced print of a painting by Spanish artist Bruno Amadio was extremely popular nationwide in the 1980s, and many households had a copy. On 4 September 1985, a fireman reported to the *Sun* newspaper that in every burning building he attended in Yorkshire, one artefact seemed to emerge unscathed – the picture of *The Crying Boy*. Ever since then it has been claimed that *The Crying Boy* is cursed, and rumoured that the majority of households which owned the paintings were burnt to the ground.

The scare caused by media sensationalism spawned weeks of mass hysteria, in which people felt the urge to burn their paintings. I certainly don't recall my mum and dad pulling the picture down from their wall and rushing to their back garden to set fire to it, but what this scare did prove was how people were affected by rumours. Many people came forward to report that any ill luck experienced by them and their family was the result of owning one of *The Crying Boy* paintings. People hysterically began questioning the purpose of the painting, asking why the boy was crying.

Newspapers asked, 'Why would people own a picture of someone crying?'

Some people caught up in the panic believed that the house fires were the result of revenge sought by the unhappy child! According to a feature in *Fortean Times* magazine, 'Roy Vickery, secretary of the Folklore Society, was quoted to the effect that the original artist may have mistreated the child model in some way ...'

The urban legend of *The Crying Boy* was absolute lunacy, with the widespread anxiety and fear provoking several fire departments, nationwide, to issue statements dismissing the connection between the paintings and the fires and other bouts of ill luck. I distinctly recall several Kent families sending their 'cursed' paintings off to the *Sun* newspaper, who stated that they would happily destroy the paintings sent in by worried readers. Even today *The Crying Boy* painting instils fear. So if you happen to have one hanging up on your wall, don't forget to blame it for any disaster that occurs in your house and then tell your friends all about it afterwards ...

⬥ Born in a Bag ⬥

It is considered good luck if a baby is 'born in the bag'. My sister Vicki was born on 23 October, just after a terrible storm ripped through Kent in 1987. She was 'born in the bag', which means that she was born with an intact amniotic sac – this occurs once in every 1,000 births. Being born *en caul* is also referred to as 'having a veil at birth'.

Legend states that if the caul is preserved then that person will never die of drowning. In the nineteenth century, it was believed that if a caul was passed on then the protective powers would be too. According to Marc Alexander in his book *British Folklore, Myths & Legends*: 'In 1813 a caul was advertised in *The Times* for 12 guineas, a considerable sum in those days.' A slightly more eerie detail of the caul legend states that anyone who still possesses their caul in death should be buried with it, otherwise 'their ghost would return to seek them'.

Another legend claims that sailors would often take cauls aboard their ship to prevent their boats or crew from suffering misfortune. The caul is often referred to by seamen as sailors' charm. In Medieval times women would sell their cauls to seamen for huge sums of money. According to an edition of the *Collectanea* series, ships' crews often spoke of how they'd escaped shark-infested waters and ocean battles thanks to the caul. 'A recital of these escapes provoked a Kentish fisherman to remark that he must have been born with a caul, and when this fact was confirmed great interest was shown in the person, particularly when it was revealed that he was a seventh child, although not of a seventh child.'

Throughout world folklore, those 'born in a bag' are considered to have mystical powers or the potential to be psychic. However, other variations state that caulbearers – especially twins – are demonic; in another version, caulbearing twins are perceived as angels.

✦ Elusive Treacle Mines ✦

According to Wikipedia:

> Treacle mining is the fictitious mining of treacle (similar to molasses) in a raw form similar to coal. The subject purports

to be serious but is an attempt to test credulity. Thick black treacle makes the deception plausible. The topic has been a joke in British humour for a century.

These mythical mines are said to be dotted around England. One treacle mine is said to exist at Tovil, in Maidstone. Many years ago, wealthy London folk would hop into their sports cars and zip down to Kent in search of such places – only to find they did not exist! Paper mills around Tovil were often called treacle mines by local folk. Wikipedia adds:

> One suggested answer to the story in this area is a rumour that the paper industry was threatened during the Second World War because there was no imported timber. Fermentation of straw was tried, creating a sticky goo. There were attempts to make paper from other than rags in the nineteenth century and an early commercial success was achieved by Samuel Hook and his son, Charles Townsend Hook, using straw at Upper Tovil Mill in the 1850s. The road next to Upper Tovil Mill became known, and was later named, as Straw Mill Hill. To produce pulp, the straw was cooked in hot alkali. After separation of the fibre, the remaining liquid looked like black treacle. Upper Tovil Mill closed in the 1980s and the site was used for a housing estate.

The mine at Tovil was even said to be haunted. A Bockingford resident reported that on certain nights 'you can still hear the ghost miners shuffling their pots … some say they still mine for the old liquid gold to this day, led by old 'Sticky Widget', treacle foreman from hell'. Treacle-mine ghosts have sometimes been described as having bulbous noses, glazed skin and sticky hair.

The village of Frittenden is also said to harbour treacle mines. In the 1930s, tourists would flock to the village to seek out the mines which, according to one local, 'produced much of the world's treacle supply'.

Another legend comes from the Strange Tales from the Dollshouse blog, which refers to a 'Treacle Tower':

> The top of the tower was sealed off in the 1950s after two local youths fell to their death whilst trying to get some 'treacle scrapings' from inside the rim of the tower. Some say the tower is haunted and that you can hear the lads' deathly wail if you press your ear firmly to the tower.

Of course, one might find it difficult to conduct a ghost hunt in a place that does not exist! Although completely unrelated, it's worth briefly mentioning a hilarious story told to me in June 2012 by a chap from Faversham, which proves how gullible members of the public can be, and how willing they are to go on a wild goose chase. After giving a talk on local legends, the gentleman told me that, many years ago, he worked for a Faversham newspaper. The team had one day decided to make up a story about a pump in the town that flowed with beer. The man said to me, 'We didn't think anyone would buy the story but imagine our shock and amusement when we looked out of the window and saw scores of people circling the pump, expecting beer to flow from it!'

✧ The Angel of Mons ✧

The Battle of Mons, which took place in Belgium in August 1914, spawned a peculiar legend. It was said that as British troops fought the enemy, angels appeared in the sky over the battlefield to spur on the Brits. Researchers claim that the origins of this 'supernatural' intervention came from the pen of Welsh author Arthur Machen. On 29 September 1914, Machen wrote a short story called 'The Bowmen', which he submitted to the *Evening News* of London. This fictional tale was set during the outbreak of war, and described phantom bowmen which aided the British in defeating the enemy. At the time of its publication, 'The Bowmen' was not branded as fiction and so many people wrote to Machen asking him to provide evidence that spectral archers supported British troops. There had clearly been some confusion and yet from this the urban legend known as the Angel of Mons was born. Through rumour alone, the bowmen of the tale became angelic figures of hope, and on 15 April 1915 *Spiritualist* magazine wrote of the heavenly intervention as if it was true. In some versions, storytellers wrote of luminous clouds said to have appeared in the sky, but certainly the most popular version concerned angels.

Despite being the product of urban legend, people actually came forward to say that they'd seen angels in the sky shortly before both the First and Second World Wars ended. One of these people was my great-grandmother Lily Lydia, who told my grandfather that whilst living in Chatham, she had seen a huge angel appear in the sky over the Coney Banks. People would often stand at this spot and watch fighter planes in combat. Knowing her character, I have no reason to disbelieve her story. These sightings were confirmed in the *South London Times* of 8 September 1944, when residents of Peckham reported seeing a similar majestic figure.

The Angel of Mons may have been dismissed as hallucination, but … step forward a former member of the German Intelligence Service, Colonel Friedrich Herzenwirth. In the

1930s, Herzenwirth told the *New York Mirror* that the eerie images were very much real; they were projections cast onto clouds by the Germans. In the case of the Battle of Mons, such 'motion pictures' were projected onto clouds by way of cinematographic machines attached to German planes. The figures were projected to cause 'superstitious terror in the Allied ranks calculated to cause panic and a refusal to fight', but this plan backfired as troops, and members of the public, perceived them as good luck, which spurred them on and gave hope in times of distress.

✧ Ghosts as Urban Legends ✧

Ghosts: half-hinted, shadowy forms seen out of the corner of an unsuspecting eye on a dark and stormy night. Phantom monks in ruined abbeys; ghostly soldiers on sites where battles took place. A spectral nurse in an old hospital; a child in Victorian attire scuttling around a shop. Ghosts seem to be everywhere, experienced by hundreds – if not thousands – of people each year. For every encounter reported, there are a handful which aren't. Some tales concern fleeting apparitions which are never seen again, whilst other ghostly legends have lasted for many years. Some of these, as in the case of the hitch-hiker, have been passed down as urban legends, twisting and changing with the times to fit the current climate. The majority of ghost stories can be taken with a pinch of salt, but others may be experienced by more than just one person. Does it take a susceptible or psychic person to see a wraith? Does a ghost still appear if there is no one there to see it? These are questions that will probably never be answered, because no one knows for sure if ghosts really exist; our only evidence is the occasional blurry photograph, or detail passed on from a medium or ghost-hunter. Even so, ghost stories have power, and some are so potent that they become embedded in the folklore and history of a place.

Blue Bell Hill isn't the only village in Kent to harbour a ghost or two. The village of Pluckley, at Ashford, has been considered Britain's most haunted village for several decades, and its ghost stories have become urban legends. The village, mentioned in the Domesday Book of the eleventh century, is quaint and rural; like most villages it has a country pub, a school and a church – and more than just a few spirits, which have attracted thousands of ghost-hunters over the years. The spectral tales seem to date back to the 1950s and concern twelve (sometimes thirteen or fourteen, depending who you talk to!) specific spirits:

1) The Highwayman

Many years ago, this unfortunate chap was speared to a tree by a sword. His darkly clad spectre has haunted the area known as Fright Corner ever since, and his dying screams are said to still reverberate around the spot.

2) The Miller

A nineteenth-century windmill used to stand on the opposite side of the B2077, and a chap named Richard (or Dicky) Buss allegedly resided there in the 1930s. Sadly, Mr Buss had the windmill closed down when it became unstable due to its age, and in 1939 it burned to the ground after being struck by lightning during a severe storm. Over the years people have reported seeing a ghostly figure in the area. Some people have even claimed that, when the windmill was a ruin, a fleeting ghost could be observed. But no one is quite sure who haunts the spot – maybe it is Dicky Buss returning to his former residence.

3) The Monk

Most haunted villages seem to have a spectral monk. This particular figure is said to haunt a house known as Greystones in the village, although the monk may have originated from the area in the twelfth century. The house was built in the 1800s, and the resident spook, although rarely sighted, is said to have connections with Pluckley's fourth spectre, the Tudor Lady.

4) The Tudor Lady

Said to haunt a building called Rose Court which is situated on the Bethersden Road, this female phantom was rumoured to have had liaisons with the monk of Greystones – though this seems highly unlikely, as they appear to be from two different periods in time. The Tudor Lady would have died sometime between 1485 and 1603 – 200 years before Greystones. She was possibly the mistress of a son of one of the Lords Dering.

5) The Screaming Man

This is a rather vague spirit from Pluckley, said to haunt an unconfirmed area in the village which once housed a brickworks. A man was said to have fallen into a clay-hole whilst working, and his screams are still heard today.

6) The Watercress Woman

This spectre is said to haunt an area known as the Pinnock Stream. The ghost is of an old gypsy woman who would, to earn her living, gather watercress from the stream and sell it on the streets. The woman died from smoking and drinking – but not in the way you would imagine. It is said that due to the alcohol spillages on her cloak, she literally went up in flames when she dropped a cigarette on herself.

7) *The White Lady of St Nicholas Church*

The wife of Lord Dering is said to haunt the churchyard of St Nicholas; her final resting place is the family vault situated inside the church.

8) *The White Lady of Surrenden Manor*

This is possibly the same spirit as that which haunts the church. Lady Dering was said to have been extremely beautiful and died at an early age. Her ghost reportedly loiters in Surrenden Manor.

9) *The Red Lady*

Another spectre of St Nicholas Church. This figure, adorned in a red gown, haunts the churchyard and was said, by marriage, to have belonged to the Dering family. The mournful spook searches amongst the crooked gravestones for her deceased child.

10) *The Schoolmaster*

In the 1920s several schoolchildren, walking near a field along Dicky Buss's Lane, discovered the body of one of their masters hanging from a tree. The spectre can still be seen swinging from the creaking branches ... on dark and stormy nights of course.

11) *The Colonel*

The wood, once known as Park Wood, no longer exists in the village but the area was once the haunt of a colonel who hanged himself in a thicket.

12) Coach and Horses

There's nothing more atmospheric than the possibility of a phantom coach and horses gliding, or even rumbling, through a rain-soaked village on a thundery night. This ghost manifests itself in and around the village. The coach is said to be drawn by four horses – sometimes headless. Other legends claim that there is only one horse.

These are the twelve ghosts of Pluckley often spoken about in ghostly tomes, ghost-hunting websites and the like. There are of course a few other ghosts around the village, which often get thrown into the Pluckley chart of chills. The Black Horse public house, situated on The Street, is said to harbour a handful of ghosts, including the spirit of a young girl. The churchyard is said to be haunted by a phantom white dog. Meanwhile, the Blacksmith's Arms is home to the ghost of a cavalier and a small boy. The Dering Arms is haunted by an old woman who sits at a table by a certain window. There is also a stretch of woodland in the village called the Screaming Woods.

In my book *Haunted Ashford*, I delved into Pluckley's classic legends and showed how such stories have become urban myths, passed down through generations despite the fact that the ghosts have rarely, if ever, been seen. Most of the sightings are so old that the majority of spooks are surely dormant, if they existed at all. As the stories are well known, any tourist or brave ghost-hunter can look up and visit the reputedly haunted sites.

Oddly, when writing of the village in the 1940s, author Charles Igglesden mentions not a single spectre, but ghost-hunter Frederick Sanders speaks of a selection a mere decade later. Some believe that most of the ghostly legends were invented by a resident of the village – possibly a chap named Desmond Carrington, who claims that the ghosts were made up for an article, to be written by journalist Bill Evans and submitted to the *Radio Times*.

Considering how old the village of Pluckley is, one would expect it to be haunted. And yet, as in the case of the phantom hitch-hiker of Blue Bell Hill, one would be pushed to actually find a witness to most of the classic twelve ghosts. Those who have come forward to report their sightings are few and far between. Despite this, Pluckley's 'twelve ghosts' still enable the village to maintain its title of 'most haunted'.

I know of no one who has seen the ghost of the Miller, the Colonel, the Monk, the Schoolmaster, the Tudor Lady, the Screaming Man or either White Lady in recent times. There seems to have been at least one case concerning a sighting of the spectral coach and horses, and the same could be said of the Highwayman, but again, these cases are rare. The ghostly Watercress Woman also seems more reclusive now than when she was alive, the only recent activity around the Pinnock Stream being a pinkish mist – hardly fitting of the bonnet-wearing, flaming gypsy woman. Strange activity has most certainly been reported at the Black Horse pub – and also surrounding public houses such as Mundy Boys and Elvey Farm – and other Pluckley residents have reported an array of supernatural encounters, and yet none of these seem able to push their way into Pluckley's top twelve ghosts. The screaming in the Screaming Woods could be blamed on foxes – or an elusive puma – and sightings of the Red Lady have only been fleeting, but in the case of Pluckley I think it's fair to say that anything unusual is immediately connected to the nearest haunted spot.

The villagers and parish council of Pluckley have, to some extent, become rather tired of the ghosts – mainly due to the fact that every Halloween groups of visitors, who seem keen to start off in the pub first, rampage through the tranquil village expecting to see the twelve ghosts of Pluckley. So severe has the nuisance become that Halloween has been banned from the village over the last few years.

Pluckley's ghosts are classic urban legends because they refuse to go away. Most of the stories don't really add up, but ghost-hunters do not always care about inaccuracies or inconsistencies. It's interesting to note another minor urban legend attached to the village, which comes from the pages of *Fortean Times*, although their source was not credited. In Issue 22 it is stated that the village 'has 13 ghosts … it also has at least 13 broken marriages from the last few years'. According to the magazine: 'Locals blame it on spectral interference, though there seems to be no direct evidence of a connection.' The small article concludes: 'But in a village that numbers the Screaming Man amongst its spectral inhabitants, perhaps it's not surprising there's a little tension in the air …'

Another ghost story that has always intrigued me concerns the ghostly fiddler of Aylesford Priory. The priory, which is home to an order of Carmelite monks and is situated a few miles short of Maidstone, has a few ghost stories attached but only one seems to have become a popular urban legend. When I first read of the phantom fiddler I was sure that the tale belonged only to Aylesford – how wrong I was. To an extent, I was saddened that the following ghost story turned out to be nothing more than an urban myth, rather than an obscure ghost yarn.

Charles Igglesden recorded that beneath Aylesford Priory are several tunnels which worm their way to a number of hidden rooms. People were rather hesitant to venture into the darkness but a brave local fiddler came forth who wanted to prove once and for all that the mysterious passageways were not all they were rumoured to be. So, one evening, with a small audience, the fiddler told the crowd, 'When I enter I will start to play my fiddle and as I proceed through the darkness you will trace me by the sound,' and with that he stepped into the eerie blackness, all the while playing his fiddle. Within a few minutes, however, the onlookers stood aghast as the fiddle seemed to screech and was then followed by a deafening silence. The fiddler never responded to any calls and the crowd were too afraid to venture into the tunnel. So the entrance was eventually bricked up, and the ghostly fiddler is said to haunt the blackness from which he never escaped.

A great ghost story, I thought, until I read an almost exact version from Hertfordshire involving a chap named Blind George who would entertain customers of the Chequers Inn at Anstey by playing his fiddle. Legend has it that one afternoon the locals were speaking of a nearby cave known as the Devil's Hole. The cave stretched for a mile underground and led to the spot where an ancient castle once stood. The passageway was simply rumour because no one was bold enough to walk the mile-long route, but Blind George would have none of it and announced that he had no need for light, and had no fear of darkness, and would venture into the cave to dispel the myth. The local folk accompanied George to the mouth of the cave and the man entered the blackness, all the while playing his fiddle. The further he went into the cave, the fainter his fiddle whine became, until suddenly the ears of the villagers were met by a petrified scream followed by a blazing spectacle, as George, consumed by fire, came running out of the Devil's Hole. Such was the fear instilled in the spectators that the cave entrance was bricked up.

This story has several variations, but all versions of the legend seem to warn that no one should enter such passageways. In one version, it is said that the fiddler enters the darkness with his dog. After the scream the man is never seen again, but his dog emerges from the passage smelling of sulphur or having a charred coat.

✳ ✳ ✳

The town and former city of Rochester harbours many ghostly tales, but its most enduring concerns the castle, which, over the centuries, has seen many bloody battles. In 1264 the castle was attacked by Simon de Montfort, Earl of Leicester. At the time, a Lady Blanche de Warenne was looking down from the battlements as her lover Ralph de Capo defended the building. It seems that one of Montfort's knights, Gilbert de Clare, was eager to accost the lady and so, disguising himself in the armour of the defendants, he entered the castle and proceeded towards the resting place of Lady Blanche. Ralph de Capo observed this sly attempt and, as de Clare reached the top of the castle, he grabbed an arrow and fired it at his enemy. Tragically, the arrow struck the armour of de Clare and then diverted and embedded itself into the breast of Lady Blanche de Warenne. For many centuries the ghost of Lady Blanche has forlornly roamed the battlements, looking for her lover.

This classic ghost story has become urban legend, and somehow, despite a lack of sightings of the ghost, has remained in Rochester folklore for many centuries. Maybe this is due to the romantic aspect of the tale. Forever she searches for her sweetheart, in exactly the same way that the spectral bride-to-be of Blue Bell Hill does, stuck in limbo in that place and only seen at certain times of the year. There are even those who claim to have seen her, and have written of their encounters in a book which the castle staff keep under the desk.

Many years ago, when ghost-hunters were allowed to stay overnight in the castle to conduct investigations, some of them reported hearing the rustling of Lady Blanche's dress (they clearly did not want to say they'd simply heard the noise of leaves being disturbed by the wind!). Other witnesses claim to have heard a man shouting along one of the corridors; perhaps it's the spectre of Gilbert de Clare approaching the lady. And what about the footsteps in the area known as Lady Tower? Could they be the faint footfalls of the woman in white as she staggers, clutching the arrow at her bosom? It's also worth noting that one reason this story has survived, most certainly over the last century or so, is due to the fact that an urban legend has been created in the playground pertaining to the ghostly woman. It is said that if you ever see the woman in white on a dark night, then you will die in a year. It's no wonder that sightings of Lady Blanche de Warenne have dwindled! Mind you, those ghostly White Ladies certainly do get about.

Another lady haunts the historic town of Faversham, at a spot known as 'Diana's Walk'. The phantom – often described as headless – is said to frequent a pathway in Bysing Wood. The legend has been passed down many decades. It is said that the woman, known as Diana (according to author Griselda Cann the woman is the Roman goddess of the hunt), carries her severed head under her arm, and may have been the daughter of the couple who owned what is now known as Syndale Park. On certain nights her fiancé would walk her home, but one night she was attacked and decapitated, whilst her fiancé – said to have been the son of the vicar of Davington Church – escaped with minor injuries. Others claim that it was in fact her fiancé who beheaded her.

Ghostly Diana, just like Lady Blanche, is now said to haunt the places she frequented in life. The haunted path runs from Davington to Judd's Folly, although this area is now houses. It is said that priests blessed these properties, possibly as a way to deter the wraith, although this has never been verified. Some claim that the legend is nothing more than a yarn created by local smugglers who operated along the nearby creeks. However, in June 2011 I spoke to a Faversham resident who claimed that around thirty years ago she, and some family members, saw the spectre of Diana's Walk whilst they were travelling on a dark road near Bysing Wood. The woman told me, 'We all saw it – a figure in white that crossed the road – it was very strange, a cold atmosphere suddenly descended upon us, the car stalled, and this figure materialised.'

Faversham is one of Kent's most haunted towns and a place which harbours some very weird legends. A spectral fox is said to prowl near to the local railway line, but one of the more disturbing urban legends claims that on certain nights at Sheldwich a bizarre half-goat/half-dog apparition is seen. Legend has it that many years ago a local woman – who may have been a witch – owned this abominable beast. She was persecuted for her alleged diabolical dabbling but her ghost, accompanied by the wretched creature, is said to still wander this realm. A spectral coach, belonging to an Old Man Smith, also travels through the town. On moonlit nights it is said that no one should look out of their windows because the ghostly coach, drawn by four horses, is on the move.

* * *

In Rochester there is a ghostly legend pertaining to author Charles Dickens, who spent many days visiting the town whilst residing at neighbouring Chatham. He even wished to be buried in the grounds of the castle moat, though in the event he was interred at Westminster Abbey. One urban legend states that on Christmas Eve, or New Year's Eve (depending on who you hear the story from!), his spectre can be seen, usually around midnight, under the moon-faced clock of the Corn Exchange. The spirit is said to be setting a pocket watch in accordance with the time on the Corn Exchange clock. Despite this being a well-known legend, I know of no one who has seen this spectre. Maybe people coming out of one of the nearby pubs – under the influence of a different type of spirit – have observed a fleeting shadow that they assumed was Dickens, but this tale is very much urban myth. So is the rumour that Dickens' ghost has been seen in the castle moat and the churchyard next to the cathedral.

Another festive phantom is Anne Boleyn, who is said to appear on Christmas Eve on a bridge that straddles the moat of Hever Castle. Anne spent much of her youth at the castle, which is situated near Edenbridge. The ghost of Anne Boleyn is said to haunt several sites throughout England – she must be a very busy spectre indeed.

The Coopers Arms public house, which can be found on St Margaret's Street in Rochester, also has a ghostly legend. This lovely pub may well be the oldest in Kent, dating back to around the eleventh century. Should you visit the pub on a warm summer's day or on a frost-bitten Christmas Eve, then be sure to look out for the figure of a monk standing behind a glass case to the right of the Kings Bar. Centuries ago, monks resided in the area and made their own wine and ales; legend has it that one monk upset his brotherhood by having an illicit affair with a local woman. As punishment, he was bricked up in the cellar of the pub and his ghost is now said to haunt the place. This ghost story has been passed down through generations and is mentioned in various books, and yet a cloaked spectre hasn't been seen for many years. The current staff have not seen the ghost but, as is the case with many allegedly haunted pubs, the creaking floorboards and swinging tankards have to be blamed on someone … or something! It's also worth mentioning another monk-related urban legend, also from Rochester. The Vines, a beautiful walkway just a few hundred yards from the pub, used to be home to the wooden figure of a monk carved from a tree. Local schoolchildren would often be spooked by this imposing figure, and any unaware person walking through The Vines of a night would no doubt be frightened by it too. The urban legend states that the figure moves at certain times of the year and has even been known to spin round – possibly to keep an eye on those loitering in the area. Sadly, at the time of writing, the monk has been cut down due to a disease eating away the trunk.

On certain nights of the year (often around November time, when the hour is late) – if you are lucky, or possibly unlucky – you will see a peculiar ghostly scene replayed. The front door of Restoration House (situated on Crow Lane in Rochester) opens and a woman dressed in white, and holding a dead baby at her breast, is said to emerge. She runs across the road into The Vines. From there she takes to Minor Canon Row and vanishes at a certain spot. A few seconds later, a monk is said to follow and vanish on the same spot. I feel for any faint-hearted soul who experiences this haunting scene under the glare of a full moon. It is a story reminiscent of a ghostly urban legend from Chilham, a charming village near Canterbury. It is said that a vicarage once stood here, where, according to Charles Igglesden:

> ... on stormy nights, so runs the tale, there may be seen issuing from the door a cowled monk carrying a flame in his hands which, with painful struggles, he keeps alive till he reaches the entrance to the churchyard. There he is confronted by a skeleton horse, which advances step by step, the monk retiring backwards till he reaches the old vicarage door, when the flame expires and monk and horse are seen no more.

I grew up with another Chilham legend. My dad always told me that Chilham Castle, which can be found off the delightful village square, was the resting (or should that be unresting!) place of a medieval woman who had been bricked up alive in the walls of the old building. I loved this story but didn't believe in it one iota – until I was researching Chilham ghosts for *Haunted Ashford*. I discovered that during the fourteenth century a woman had allegedly been bricked up in the tower, and that her spectre had been seen in the ladies' powder room which sits beneath the spot. It may be coincidence, but staff and visitors alike have reported seeing a woman in an old-fashioned dress floating around the place, and many years ago workmen discovered skeletons chained to a wall.

The town of Chatham has a creepy urban legend attached to it which comes from the historic dockyard on Dock Road. Chatham Dockyard is possibly one of Kent's most haunted locations, but the story of the ghostly drummer boy is sure to send a shiver down even the most hardened of spines. The nearby Fort Amherst lays claim to 'owning' the ghostly legend; their version of events is incorrect, but proves how urban legends can get twisted out of shape or tied to a certain location to which they did not originally belong.

Many people say they have heard about the drummer boy ghost. The story claims that a young boy, serving at the barracks, was accosted on the Great Lines (or local marshes) by two Royal Marines and robbed. The boy was then beheaded, his body dumped, and his head put inside his own drum and entombed within a chimney at the barracks. His spectre – often headless – has been observed marching through the Fort, and in the 1960s it was rumoured that during an excavation at the barracks the drum, containing the skull of the boy, was found. This is the story that many people have heard, especially on ghost tours of Fort Amherst, a popular attraction. And yet it is far removed from the grisly truth.

Pam Wood, who runs ghost tours at Chatham Dockyard, has looked into the history of the drummer boy story and has uncovered a wealth of information that proves once and for all how the story came to be, and, whilst a murder did take place, it was more complex than the eerie legend. On 30 June 1872, drummer boy George Stock was sitting in the Royal Marine Library (now Gun Wharf), reading a newspaper, when he had his throat slit by Royal Marine James Tooth. It is believed that Tooth had lent the teenager some money – something deemed illegal within the establishment – and been told off for this by senior officers. So, on Sunday 30 June, possibly in a drunken rage, he killed the boy. Tooth fled the scene with blood on his hands, leaving Stock to stagger downstairs, where he collapsed on the parade ground. Initially Tooth denied killing Stock, but after severe interrogation he finally confessed. He was kept at Maidstone Jail – where he commented that the image of the boy (but not the ghost) haunted him – and he was eventually executed on 13 August.

Pam Wood believes the drummer boy story is one of 'oral tradition'; a tale passed down through military history which has never been confined to an exact location. One of the only recorded encounters with the wraith concerns a vicar of nearby St Mary's Church, who may have seen the apparition near the sentry gate, but there is no date for this sighting. The details of the skull in the drum are most certainly myth, and it's likely that the current story doing the rounds is completely inaccurate. It's also interesting to note that Dover Castle has a similar legend pertaining to a young drummer named Sean, who was allegedly killed for the money he was carrying and beheaded.

One last urban legend I'd like to share with you concerning Fort Amherst revolves around what is known as the Angel Stone, a peculiar scarred stone that can be found in one of the main passageways upon entering the fort. Many years ago it was rumoured that Napoleonic soldiers carved out the fort passageways we see today (although it's more likely that Welsh miners dug out the tunnels) and that the Angel Stone was often touched for good luck as they prepared for a day – or night – underground. The strange carving on the stone, which some people believe to be an angel, could simply be aimless scratch marks.

Another Kent location that can almost guarantee a scare is Reculver. This coastal village sits about three miles east of Herne Bay, and in AD 43 the Romans built a fort here. Eventually this fort was given over to a monastery dedicated to St Mary. On certain nights, or so they say, the screams and cries of children can be heard sweeping along the coast, emanating from the remains of the church and the fort. This legend may have originated in the 1960s, when an archaeological dig unearthed several infant skeletons beneath the Roman structures. No one is quite sure why the babies were buried there; some claim that they were sacrificed, whilst others claim these babies were stillborn. Either way, the imposing towers, which overlook the sullen waters, are a remote setting perfect for a reputed haunting. Are those oft-reported cries the sound of babies breathing their last breath? Or merely the howls of an angry coastal wind?

* * *

In Strood, during a nasty argument between Thomas á Becket and Henry II, the men of the town (loyal to the King) allegedly accosted the Archbishop's horse and snipped off its tail as it passed through the town. Folklore states that Becket, rather unhappy at this, declared that any future offspring of the pranksters would be born with tails!

There is another horse-related legend in the town of Rainham, in Kent; it is known as the Bloors Coach legend. Every midnight the black, spectral coach – drawn by a team of headless horses and driven by a headless coachman who holds his head in his hands – travels through a housing estate which used to be the site of Queen Court in Berengrave Lane. The coach stops at a certain spot, where an old woman spins atop a barn, and then rumbles on to Bloors Place, where it vanishes. According to *Folklore, Myths & Legends of Britain*: 'The passenger in the coach is said to be the ghost of Christopher Bloor, who had a reputation as a ladies man in Tudor times. The legend says that the town's irate husbands banded together and waylaid him at midnight.' He supposedly suffered a grisly death at their hands – his head was cut off and put on a spike to be displayed from the church tower. However, the records of Bloor's actual death show that he died in his bed.

A festive urban legend states that every Christmas Eve the occupants of Bloor's old house used to put a glass of brandy out for him, and in the morning the alcoholic beverage had been drunk … or maybe it was Father Christmas! When the local policeman was asked about the phantom drinker, he responded, 'It is a fact but I blame the postman!'

✳ ✳ ✳

The Goodwin Sands, on the Kent coast, is a treacherous stretch of shoreline situated five or so miles off Deal. Over the years many people have perished aboard ships wrecked on these cruel waters. The most famous ghost story here concerns the *Lady Lovibond*, a three-masted schooner said to still haunt the foaming waters many years after being wrecked whilst bound for Oporto in 1748. It was considered bad luck at the time for a lady to be aboard a ship, and the sailors were all too aware of this legend, but the captain's new bride, Annetta, wished to journey alongside the crew. The biggest problem with this was the fact that also aboard the ship was a former admirer of Annetta's, who still had strong feelings for her. He killed her husband at the helm in a fit of jealousy. The ship was eventually steered onto the sands.

Ever since this tragic event, every fifty or so years, on 13 February, it is said that the phantom ship can be seen off the shore at Deal. On 13 February 1798, the master of the ship *Edenbridge* noted in his logbook that his boat had almost collided with a three-masted schooner, and there were also reports of a schooner running aground – but there was no trace. In 1848 the ghost ship was observed again, and again lifeboat men who investigated could find no trace of it. This type of incident is said to happen every fifty years but sceptics argue that it is nothing more than an urban myth. On 12 March 1969, the *Evening Post* reported: 'Ghost ship hunt after collision', following a similar incident off Dover, a neighbouring coastal town of Deal. A sea and air search was conducted in the Dover Strait after a tanker radioed to state that it had collided with 'an unknown vessel near the Goodwin Sands'. The incident took place during a heavy snowfall. According to the newspaper: 'No radio message has been picked up from the other craft which is believed to be small.'

* * *

Have you noticed how thunderstorms often play a part when it comes to telling ghost stories? Blackened skies, the crackle of lightning and the patter of rain provide an atmospheric backdrop for any chilling tale. Mind you, my next story concerns a terrifying event which took place at Great Chart in Kent, on a bright summer's day in 1613. At the Church of St Mary, vicar Hadrian Savaria was conducting a sermon when suddenly a frightful creature, reminiscent of a legendary Black Dog, appeared before the congregation. A giant, black, flaming bull – snorting and scraping its feet – materialised, sending those in attendance scattering throughout the aisles. The apparition charged the rows, causing several deaths as it crashed into the North Wall. The church filled with a nauseating odour and the garments of the vicar were severely scorched before the monster burst into a ball of flame. A terrifying episode indeed, and one which seems sporadically recorded throughout British folklore, albeit usually during severe storms. On most occasions a creature resembling a Black Dog is recorded, but sceptics and scientists like to put forward a more logical explanation – the little understood phenomenon known as ball lightning. Ball lightning often appears during, or before, a storm, and resembles a glowing ball that is able to change shape or split into other parts, scorch the interior of buildings, and then dissipate. However, such events are often exaggerated into tales of demonic entities. One such case, originating from the village of Bungay, in Suffolk, involves a ferocious Black Dog which is said to have attacked the Church of St Mary in 1577. Rumour has it that no such event occurred and that the materialisation of the fiend was invented by the local vicar – little did he realise that, many years later, his fictitious story would become local legend.

Another peculiar story which has been passed down over the years has become known as the Hairy Man of Wouldham, a village situated not far from Blue Bell Hill. In the 1960s, a young woman was told by her grandmother that if she didn't behave then the 'hairy man of Wouldham' would come and get her. When I was told about this spectre I had to laugh at such a seemingly ludicrous idea – until the woman in question stated quite categorically that this was a serious matter, and a story passed down several generations since the 1920s. According to the woman, there had been numerous sightings around the local woods of a hairy, bipedal creature, and it had become a bogeyman for kids to fear, in the same way as the Bogman and Leaf Man.

The more I investigated, the more strangeness was revealed. For instance, in the 1940s a family who resided on the Kent coast claimed to have had a bizarre encounter with a horrid, hair-covered creature, something akin to a werewolf – that man-beast of world folklore. Whilst having a picnic with her grandmother in the woods, Pat Shirley saw a creature that was 'covered in flaming red hair', and 'possessing a pair of huge and powerful jaws'. Apparently, the beast was seen only briefly before it moved off into the trees. Weirder still, a woman (who only wants to be known as Maureen) had a terrifying encounter which seemingly proves that Walderslade's sparse woodlands were at one time being stalked by an unnatural creature.

What Maureen saw, and never spoke of until she confided in me in 2006, was something quite unique. This is an experience that has remained in her mind for more than thirty years:

> I was in the woods behind Sherwood Avenue, in Walderslade in the August of 1975. I was 18 at the time and myself and my ex-husband were about to light a small fire, as it must have been around 10 p.m., quite dark. My husband was crouched down sorting the fire out and I was standing. It was then that I saw them, two piercing, reddish eyes just around ten yards away. I froze in terror, because this thing was big. It was around seven-feet in height but in the darkness I could make out the bulk of it. Its figure wasn't like that of a man, it was a mass, a hulking figure, like it was hairy. I really thought I'd seen the Devil!

I was unnerved and yet intrigued by the horror in her voice.

> I just stood there and then it seemed to lower, quite slowly
> and after a few seconds it disappeared behind heavy foliage,
> but I could sense it was still there. I immediately made excuses
> to leave and we did, and I kept that terrifying night with me
> and never spoke to anyone.

What on earth had Maureen seen that night? Was it just someone in a gorilla suit? In the early 1990s, five men belonging to the Territorial Army had a similar encounter with what they described as a man-beast in the village of Burham. I find it intriguing that so many of these man-beast legends take place in Blue Bell Hill or the neighbouring villages.

A woman named Corriene, who lives in Maidstone, had an encounter in around 2003 in the vicinity of Kit's Coty House at Blue Bell Hill. Corriene, who has psychic ability, was in the area with some friends when she saw a figure marching aggressively towards her uphill. The figure was robust and seemed to be covered in hair, but as it got closer she realised that it was wearing rabbit skins around its waist and furred boots on its feet; it appeared to be a Neolithic hunter, with long hair and heavily bearded. According to Corriene, this man was not flesh and blood but some type of spectral warrior from the past.

These stories sounded extremely unusual, and yet as a child I grew up influenced by a 1980s television series, based on a 1960s book, called *Stig of the Dump*. The story concerns a boy called Barney who, whilst visiting his grandmother, visits a local quarry and slips, ending up meeting a caveman of sorts whom he names Stig. Stig has a den in the chalk quarry, wears a cloth around his waist, and has a great deal of hair on his body. I was intrigued that Kent had been mentioned in the book and wondered if the work had been based on Blue Bell Hill and its man-beast legends. I was further fascinated when I found out that the television series had been filmed at Blue Bell Hill. Perhaps the producers, or the author Clive King (who spent much of his life in Kent), had grown up with legends about the old hill. A mysterious set of standing stones are also mentioned in both the book and film, as well as an encounter with an escaped leopard! Was all this coincidence or do the urban legends have some basis in reality? I guess we'll never know. It is worth noting that in medieval folklore there are several mentions of 'wild men', or the woodwose – a mythical figure that often appears in literature and artwork from medieval Europe. They were often perceived as nature sprits, in the same way as the satyr or faun. Such figures also appeared in the carved works of cathedrals, such as Canterbury. So, maybe that woman from Wouldham was right, and if you don't behave the hairy man *will* get you.

I'm sure that meeting a wild man or phantom drummer boy on a remote stretch of road on a pitch-black night would be unsettling enough, but surely the very last paranormal entity you would want to encounter is the Grim Reaper – Death himself. There are many urban legends featuring the figure of Death. However, some people claim to have had an actual encounter with such a foreboding figure.

Martin, an antiques dealer from Rainham, said:

It was about three o' clock in the morning … It was July 2006, a particularly humid night, and I couldn't drop off to sleep. I was tossing and turning, trying to get comfortable … and then I saw it. I say 'it' but I knew what it was. It was the Grim Reaper. I had rolled over and my gaze was met by a black garment, a cloak of sorts, and I ran my eyes up the body of the figure, and noted two skeletal hands and the black hood. This was no dream, but, like a child I turned away in fright, and cowered under the blankets until dawn came.

A few weeks after this terrifying encounter, Martin lost his father. He believes, to this day, that the Reaper had come as a warning. This wasn't the first time the Hooded One had appeared to someone in Kent. In 1999, a Kent woman named Missy had been to visit her grandmother in Maidstone. She was accompanied by her mother and younger sister. Missy's mother was driving the car and as they came out of the road where her grandmother lived, Missy's mum stopped to give way to some traffic. When Missy looked to her right she saw a figure in a black robe and hood, holding a scythe. In the blink of an eye the figure vanished.

'If it had been somebody in a fancy dress costume I would have seen them run away,' stated Missy in 2011. The Reaper was no belated Halloween prank either, because the sighting had taken place in broad daylight in the summer! Missy's sister also saw the figure, asking, 'Who was that?' before going on to describe exactly the same apparition.

'To this day I don't know why I saw it,' said Missy, 'but I remain absolutely convinced that what I saw was real.'

Although not many encounter this hooded spectre, we know what it looks like and why it appears. It is a figure that has been introduced to our living rooms by way of literature and television. A classic example of the Reaper is the final wraith to visit Ebenezer Scrooge in Charles Dickens' *A Christmas Carol*. The cloaked figure exists as a warning that if you don't change your mean and miserly ways then chances are you'll end up in an early grave. The Grim Reaper has often been given a negative image. Although it appears as a tall, thin, shadowy ghoul, it may exist to help us avoid a moment of misfortune, or somehow prepare us for a forthcoming death. Either way, its empty face has become embedded in folklore as an urban legend.

* * *

My last spook legend concerns Frederick Sanders, a local ghost-hunter who, around half a century ago, investigated many reputedly haunted properties and locations. He spoke of a fascinating and grisly urban legend from the River Swale, at a spot rather ghoulishly named Dead Man's Island (not to be confused with St Mary's Island in Chatham, which was also given the eerie title after the remains of Napoleonic soldiers were unearthed there). In June 1950, Sanders, accompanied by fellow journalist Duncan Rand, conducted a midnight trip at the 'island of ghosts', a point where the River Medway meets the Swale. French soldiers had been buried here centuries ago after being taken prisoner by the British. They had succumbed to the terrible conditions and the bubonic plague.

According to the local rumour, many of the coffins were bereft of their lids and, as Sanders noted, none of the skeletons were in possession of a skull. Stranger still, none of the skulls were ever found on the island, suggesting that someone – or something – had removed them. Sanders noted an urban legend which had circulated around the villages, with locals claiming that the reason for the absence of skulls was the presence of an abhorrent ghost hound which, shortly after the burial of the soldiers, on a moonless night, prowled the stuffy burial ground and raided the coffins, and with razor-sharp fangs prised open the skulls to feast on the brains of the dead.

It's no wonder that Sanders and Rand were nervous of visiting an area known as Coffin Bay. Thankfully for the intrepid explorers, the nearest they got to experiencing anything untoward was the eerie mist that danced upon the water. Meanwhile, several wooden stakes driven into the mud in the distance looked like black warriors rising from some weedy nether realm. No sign, however, of the ghastly skull-cracking hound of Hell.

✳ ✳ ✳

In order to ward off evil spirits, people would often hide shoes in places such as the fireplace, chimney, under floorboards, behind walls and up in the roof. A restaurant in Rochester was going through refurbishment a few years ago when the owner came across a small child's shoe in the fireplace. Most people would jump to the conclusion that the shoe had simply been lost by a child or misplaced by the family, but, after investigating, the manager came to believe that it had been placed in a certain spot to deter demons. The shoe has never left the building. Be careful what you throw away when clearing out that old building you've just moved into!

◇ 'Waiter, there's a fly in my soup!' ◇

In the *Chatham Standard* of 4 February 1975, a horrifying headline read: 'Woman killed by pin in lump of meat.' The story concerned a sixty-nine-year-old pensioner from Glencoe Road, Chatham, who haemorrhaged after swallowing a metal pin, measuring some 1¼in in length. The woman died a few days afterwards, not realising that she was bleeding internally.

Normally, this type of horror story is confined to urban legend. Jan Harold Brunvand, in his book *The Vanishing Hitch-hiker*, calls these legends 'The Kentucky Fried Rat And Other Nasties'. He comments: 'A number of recurrent stories deal with food contamination, always a real possibility, even with our country's strict regulations of quality control.'

If there's one legend that often merges with fact then it's the Strange Object in Food tale, or, to give it another name, Waiter! There's a Fly in my Soup! In January 2007, *BBC News* reported: 'Stone found in baby food tin', after a Maidstone couple discovered a peculiar hard object in a tin of spaghetti Bolognese which they were feeding their eleven-month-old daughter. It was rumoured that a Margate family had found a metal shard in the same product previously.

Jan Harold Brunvand states: 'Very few – if any – folk informants ever have a news clipping about foreign matter in food to back up their claims that the story they know is a true one.' But as you've just read, he is incorrect. Whilst there are many stories passed down regarding strange things being found in food and drink, it would seem that quite a few of these incidents are actually fact. I recall that in the 1980s and 1990s, many people from the Medway Towns moaned about a certain takeaway 'down the road' or 'in the High Street' that was serving up rats and mice in its food. A more dramatic urban legend claimed that one particular restaurant was responsible for the disappearance of several small dogs in the area and were using dog meat. It's no wonder so many people panicked, even though most of these stories were unfounded

– as were the rumours that some products purchased from supermarkets could give you cancer and goodness knows what else. This reminds me of a rabies scare going round in the 1980s. Rabies was a greatly feared disease at the time, but the majority of folk didn't understand a thing about it and were force-fed information by newspapers. If I recall correctly, much of the hysteria was caused by too many people watching the 1983 horror movie *Cujo*, in which a rabid St Bernard dog traps a woman and her young son in their car.

Regarding the food scares, the *Telegraph* of 13 October 2011 reported: 'Bizarre urban myth ruining business at Chinese restaurant', with reporter Richard Alleyne commenting on the unfounded scares pertaining to foreign items and unusual animals being used secretly in food. He wrote: 'The rumour, which began on the Internet, is becoming so widespread that a 30-year-old restaurant could go out of business.'

The damaging legend – which certainly began long before the Internet existed – doesn't just claim that people are unknowingly eating dog meat, but that in some cases customers are choking on dog tags and microchips rumoured to have come from missing pets. The urban legends reference website Snopes reports that the legend of The Cat in the Chinese Food is completely false, and comments that the myth 'has been traced by British researchers to the earliest years of the British Empire in England and to the 1850s in the United States'.

Even so, people do occasionally find weird things in their grub. On 3 September 2010, the *Independent* reported: 'Rat found in tin of baked beans.' This was echoed by a similar headline from the *Dartford Messenger* of 14 October the same year: 'Rat's tail found in Big Mac', after a twenty-nine-year-old man claimed to have discovered the foreign item when about to nibble on his favourite fast-food meal. In 2002 it was claimed that a Chatham chef had been fined after mouse droppings were found in food served up by his restaurant. In another incident, a woman claimed that she'd found a piece of metal in her food whilst dining in Ramsgate. And a few years ago a group of teenage girls claimed that they'd found a 'scab' in their fish and chips, whilst a Maidstone woman reported she'd found glass in her bowl of cereal!

On 6 July 2011, Kent Online reported the rather nauseating story of a toenail being found in a pizza in Sittingbourne. On Friday 13th (of all days!) 2006, *Sky News* reported that a needle had been discovered in a loaf of bread at Orpington. Shards of glass had also been found, suggesting malicious tampering. However, the most alarming story from Kent was reported by Kent Online on 9 February 2012, under the headline: 'Snake horror as Cheryl Lowrey finds corn snake in a tortilla wrap.' The website commented: 'Cheryl, 35, felt something unusual inside the packet when she picked it up from her kitchen cupboard. Wondering what it was she took a look inside and shrieked when she saw the orange corn snake curled up on the half-eaten wrap.'

I discovered a few more strange headlines, in reference to alien objects in food, in copies of the *Chatham Standard* from the early 1980s. These included: 'A bolt in a pasty', 'mice droppings in sugar', 'animal remains found in beans', 'matchstick found in fish and chips' and, my favourite, 'Woodlice found in policeman's chips'.

So, there you have it, urban legends pertaining to food aren't always fiction. So be careful when sitting down to eat your favourite meal!

✦ Licking legends! ✦

There's an American story which has found its way to English shores over the years. I heard it in a pub from a woman named Sharon Miller in 1993, who was telling a group of friends a story about her friend Pamela. According to Sharon, Pamela went to stay at a friend's house in Canterbury and took her dog with her. One night, Pamela was in the house alone and heard on the radio that there was a deranged guy roaming the ill-lit roads, preying on women. Rather spooked by this news, Pamela made sure that all the windows and doors were locked and retired to bed. Her dog, a Yorkshire terrier, slept under the bed. In the middle of the night, according to Sharon anyway, Pamela awoke to the sound of dripping, and thought that maybe the bathroom tap hadn't been turned off tightly enough. But she didn't want to get out of bed as she was too cosy. To reassure herself, Pamela felt under the bed for her dog, and was calmed when the terrier licked her hand. She then dozed off. Pamela awoke twice more in the night, never once bothering to turn the tap off properly. In the morning, to her horror, she awoke to find her small dog hanging from the bathroom door, its throat cut, blood dripping on the lino. And worst of all there was a note, drawn in blood on the door, which said: 'Humans Can Lick Too.'

According to Sharon, the lunatic on the loose had broken into the house, killed the dog, and lain in wait under the bed, and every time Pamela reached down for the 'dog', the sadist had licked her hand.

This urban legend is often referred to as The Licked Hand, and is completely untrue. There are several versions of this story, and the biggest frustration for me, after speaking to Sharon, was the fact that I could not get her to contact Pamela. Sharon claimed that Pamela had moved away after the incident, and I didn't have the heart to tell her that Pamela, or whoever Pamela had heard the story from, had completely made it up!

* * *

Another Licking Legend is a well-known office myth. I recall a local newspaper some years ago – I'm not sure which newspaper – reporting that a firm in the Dover or Deal area was in panic after office staff reported feeling ill and vomiting after licking a batch of envelopes. The rumour doing the rounds was that the envelopes had been laced – probably in the factory they were made – with poison. In other cases it has been claimed that eggs from an insect were found on some envelopes and those who licked them became ill. I'm surprised the eggs never hatched and the insects didn't live happily ever after in the stomachs of the victims! One version of the story I heard is that a woman got a paper cut on her tongue and a few weeks later her tongue began to swell. When she went to the doctor, the protuberance began to move and then split, revealing a pus-covered insect.

✧ 'Does it really rain cats and dogs?' ✧

Rumours of dog parts being found in restaurant meals seem far-fetched, but what about tales of dogs and cats falling from the sky? The phrase 'It's raining cats and dogs' simply means it is raining severely, and there appears to be no definitive origin for the saying. Some believe the phrase dates back several centuries and may have concerned a torrential downpour somewhere that literally washed cats and dogs from rooftops of buildings. This is complete nonsense and an urban legend in itself, but there have certainly been peculiar downpours in Kent which keep the legend alive. Many people dismiss reports of odd objects falling from the heavens, although cases regarding frogs, strange-coloured soot and sand, snails, and the occasional coin do exist. My two favourite Kent stories of unusual downpours are quite old, dating back several centuries. The first tale comes from a Mr Samuel Horsley, Bishop of Rochester, who wrote the following letter in 1797 at Bromley House in reference to a most unusual fall from the sky:

The forenoon of this day (10 July) was remarkably sultry, with little sunshine, except for about two hours and a half from noon. The greatest heat was about 3 o'clock when the sky was overcast again. At that time the Thermometer already in the shade, at a window on the north side of my house, and so fixed as to face the east, was at 81 degrees. But a little before it was taken to 77 degrees, and the Barometer at the same time, which in the morning had been at 30,08, was sunk at 30,03. Just about this time I observed the cows and Welsh poneys in my paddock all galloping towards the yard, as if something had frightened them. The sky was overcast with dark lowering clouds, the swallows were flying very low, and from many appearances I apprehended that a heavy thunderstorm was approaching. We had sitten down to dinner (perhaps about 5 or 10 minutes past four) when a young Lady at table suddenly exclaimed in great surprise, that 'the hay was all falling about the garden'. Running to the window I saw many little handfuls of hay falling gently and almost perpendicularly through the air upon my lawn. Going to the front door,

I saw the same sort of shower descending upon the grass on the contrary side of the house, and found my gardiner and labourous gazing at it. I observed a large black cloud coming over the house with a very slow motion from south to north, or nearly in that direction. Fixing my eyes steadily on the middle of that cloud, I saw several of these parcels of hay, one after another, dropping in appearance from the bosom of the cloud, and becoming first visible at a great height in the atmosphere. They descended with a very slow motion, and with a very small deviation from the perpendicular in the direction in which the cloud moved. The atmosphere all this time was remarkably close and still. Not a leaf of the trees moved, not a breath of air was stirring, and my own hay was lying motionless in the field. Towards the evening a light breeze sprang up, which soon died away again; and the whole day has passed off without thunder, rain, or storm of any kind. The specimen of this hay, which I have the honour to send you, is the aggregate of two of the little parcels picked up by myself on opposite sides of the house. [*sic*]

In another bizarre incident, from 1666, a shower of fish is recorded. The event was reported by a doctor:

On Wednesday before Easter, Anno 1666, a pasture field at Cranstead near Wrotham in Kent, about two acres, which is far from any part of the sea or branch of it, and a place where [there] are no fish ponds, but a scarcity of water, was all overspread with little fishes, conceived to be rained down, there having been at that time a great tempest of thunder and rain; the fishes were about the length of a man's little finger, and judged by all that saw them to be young whitings, many of them were taken up and shewed to several persons;

the field belonged to one Ware a Yeoman, who was at the Easter sessions one of the Grand Inquest, and carried some of them to the sessions at Maidstone in Kent, and he showed them, among others, to Mr Lake, a bencher of the Middle Temple, who had one of them and brought it to London, the truth of it was averr'd by many that saw the fishes lye scattered all over the field, and none in other fields thereto adjoining: The quantity of them was estimated to be about a Bushel, being all together. Mr Lake gave the charge at those sessions. [*sic*]

This type of shower was often dismissed as urban legend because no one could ever find a reason as to why such things would fall from the sky. Those who did believe usually blamed water spouts (giant funnels of water said to suck up certain items and then deposit them elsewhere) but this does not explain the selective manner of the phenomenon. In many cases only certain species of fish were picked up, and how do we explain the dangerous metal rod that fell on a house in Bickley in 1967? Maybe it had been dropped by an aeroplane, yet how do we explain the sudden shower of coins that clattered onto the roof of a house in Ramsgate in 1989? And the fact that these sporadic showers took place throughout a six-year period?

But if you thought fish, hay and coins were the strangest things to have ever fallen from the sky, consider one of Kent's oldest urban legends. Inhabitants of Gravesend were stunned when, during a church congregation in 1211, they observed a strange 'ship' in the clouds which released an anchor that clanked against a gravestone. Shortly afterwards it was claimed that a man 'swam' down from the ship to retrieve the anchor but to no avail, and so he returned to the craft, which went off into the clouds – but not before one of the occupants cut free the object which remained amongst the graves. So unnerved were the congregation that the vicar ushered them back into the church.

This fascinating account may sound like one of the first ever UFO sightings – if you believe such things – but it's interesting to note that this story has circulated elsewhere in Britain, suggesting it is an urban legend and nothing more. An almost identical story originated in Bristol in 1270, when it was claimed that a spaceship was seen over the area; as one of the occupants scampered down the ladder dropped from the ship, he was pelted with stones by onlookers. It seems that the man was not from this planet because he choked in the atmosphere.

Another, almost identical, version of the legend comes from the Irish borough of Cloera from AD 956 (also recorded as 1211, suggesting confusion between this and the Gravesend incident). It was claimed that a ship in the sky dropped an anchor at the Church of St Kinarus. According to the urban myth, the anchor became snagged on the door of the church and people came rushing out of the building just in time to see a man descend a ladder – panic – and then flee back inside the hull of a peculiar ship. The legend concludes that certain villagers cut the anchor free and kept it on display in the church. We also hear of a very similar tale from 1122, this time from London and chronicled by Frenchman St Peter of Vigeois.

It is truly amazing to read so many accounts describing almost the same thing. There are numerous other places in Britain which lay claim to this legend, and there's even mention of such an incident in America, but on this occasion the anchor allegedly got snagged on a railroad track.

* * *

And so there you have it, a compendium of Kent-related urban legends, tall tales, fairy stories and myths which have toured not just the county but in some cases the world, from mouth to mouth, culture to culture, and town to town – each transforming through the ages in order to fit into the current climate. That's the power of the urban legend, and whether you believe such yarns or not, you cannot deny their ability to create gossip, or even panic.

Oh, and before I go, just remember not to completely dismiss urban myths. The next time you're walking – alone – on a dark and stormy night, be careful not to grimace or poke your tongue out in order to mock the latest fable, legend or friend-of-a-friend lore, because, as my parents once told me, 'if the wind blows in the wrong direction, your face might just stay like that!'

It may be that nothing in the world is so hard to comprehend as a terror whose time has come and gone – which may be why parents can scold their children for their fear of the bogeyman, when as children themselves they had to cope with exactly the same fears ...

◆

Danse Macabre, **Stephen King**

BIBLIOGRAPHY

Folklore, Myths & Legends of Britain (Reader's Digest, 1973)

Alexander, Marc, *British Folklore, Myths & Legends* (Sutton, 2005)

Arnold, Neil, *Haunted Ashford* (The History Press, 2011)

Arnold, Neil, *Haunted Chatham* (The History Press, 2012)

Arnold, Neil, *Haunted Maidstone* (The History Press, 2011)

Arnold, Neil, *Haunted Rochester* (The History Press, 2011)

Arnold, Neil, *Mystery Animals of the British Isles: Kent* (CFZ Press, 2009)

Arnold, Neil, *Paranormal Kent* (The History Press, 2010)

Beaney, Stuart & O'Leary, Diarmuid, *Medway Towns* (Tempus, 2001)

Brunvand, Jan Harold, *The Vanishing Hitch-hiker* (Norton, 1981)

Cann, Griselda, *Ghost Stories from Faversham* (Winterwood, 1995)

Igglesden, Charles, *A Saunter through Kent with Pen and Pencil* (Kentish Express, various)

Fort, Charles, *Wild Talents* (John Brown, 1998)

Websites:

www.forteantimes.com

www.kentmonsters.blogspot.com

www.kentnews.co.uk
www.kentonline.co.uk
www.news.bbc.co.uk
www.roadghosts.com
www.snopes.com
www.strangetalesfromthedollshouse.blogspot.com
www.studentmidwife.net
www.urbanlegends.about.com
www.urbanlegendsonline.com
www.wikipedia.org

Some recommended films with urban legends as their theme:
Candyman (1992)
The Grudge (2002)
The Monkey's Paw (various)
One Missed Call (2003)
Ring (1998)
Trilogy of Terror (1976)
Urban Legend (1998)
When a Stranger Calls (1976)
When a Stranger Calls Back (1993)